CONTENTS

ALGEBRA

SETS AND SYMBOLS

A set is a collection of elements (members) and may be denoted by

1. a capital letter,
2. listing the elements in brackets,
3. describing the properties required to be an element of the set.

Here are some examples of familiar sets:

N, $\{1, 2, 3, \ldots\ldots\}$, the set of natural numbers.
Note that the series of dots indicates that the set is infinite.

W, $\{0, 1, 2, 3, \ldots\ldots\}$, the set of whole numbers.

Z, $\{\ldots, -3, -2, -1, 0, 1, 2, 3, \ldots\}$, the set of integers.

Q, $\left\{\frac{p}{q} : p, q \in Z, q \neq 0\right\}$, the set of rational numbers, e.g. $\frac{2}{3}, -\frac{3}{4}$ etc.

The section in the brackets is read '$\frac{p}{q}$ such that p, q are elements of the set Z, q is not equal to zero'.

The symbol $\in$ means 'is an element of'. The symbol $\notin$ would mean 'is not an element of'.

R, The set of real numbers. A real number is one which corresponds to any point on the number line, e.g. $7, \frac{2}{3}, -0.19, \pi, \sqrt{3}$, etc.

$\emptyset$, or $\{\ \}$, The empty set, i.e. one which has no members, e.g. the set of real roots of $x^2 = -3$.

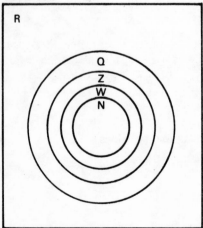

The universal set, i.e. the set which has all the elements contained in all the other sets under consideration. For example, if the set R is taken to be the universal set then all the other sets mentioned above are said to be subsets of R and may be represented in the diagram as shown here.

BASIC KNOWLEDGE REVISED 'H' GRADE MATHEMATICS

JOHN F. MORGAN

ISBN 0 7169 3140 0

ROBERT GIBSON · Publisher
17 Fitzroy Place, Glasgow, G3 7SF.

INTRODUCTION

This Basic Knowledge text is intended for those working towards the S.C.E. examination on the revised syllabus for Higher Grade Mathematics. In selecting the contents the author has closely followed the contents list issued by the Scottish Examination Board in order to ensure that the subject matter, worked examples and graphs are relevant to the examination.

It is hoped that with the aid of this text the task of the candidates preparing for the examination will be less arduous, the progress more sustained and the effort well rewarded.

John F. Morgan, 1989.

The set N is a subset of the set W and in symbols is written $N \subset W$.

If $E = \{1, 2, 3\}$ then $\{1, 2\} \subset E$.

If $A = \{2, 3\}$ then A' (the complement of A) is $\{1\}$, i.e. the set of elements in E which do not belong to A.

Some sets may have elements in common, e.g. the set of points on the line $x = 3$ and the set of points on the line $y = 4$ have only one point in common, $(3, 4)$, since they intersect at this point, so if A is the set of points on the line $x = 3$ and B is the set of points on the line $y = 4$ then $A \cap B$ (read 'A intersection B') is the set $\{(3, 4)\}$ i.e. $A \cap B = \{(3, 4)\}$.

The set of points which satisfy the inequation $(x - 2)(x + 3) > 0$ is the union of the two sets $\{x : x < -3\}$ and $\{x : x > 2\}$ i.e. $\{x : x < -3\} \cup \{x : x > 2\}$ which is shown in the diagram below.

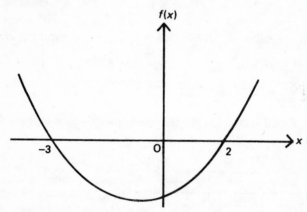

The order in which the elements of a set are listed is of no consequence thus $\{1, 2, 3\} = \{3, 1, 2\}$ but it is usually more convenient to impose some order.

Algebra

SEQUENCES

The order of the terms of a sequence, unlike that of sets, is important because there is a relationship between the consecutive terms of a sequence.

For example 2, 4, 6, 8, ... is a sequence where

the first term $u_1 = 2$
the second term $u_2 = 4$
the third term $u_3 = 6$
the nth term $u_n = 2n$

The above is a sequence of even numbers and each term is related to the next by the recurrence relation $u_{n+1} = u_n + 2$, e.g. $u_2 = u_1 + 2$, $u_3 = u_2 + 2$ etc.

The above sequence is of the form called an arithmetic sequence since there is a common difference between the consecutive terms i.e. $u_{n+1} - u_n = 2$.

In general $u_{n+1} - u_n = d$, where d is a constant, represents an arithmetic sequence.

A geometric sequence is one where there is a common ratio between consecutive terms, i.e. $\dfrac{u_{n+1}}{u_n} = r$, where r is a constant. For example in the

sequence 3, 6, 12, 24, ... $\dfrac{u_{n+1}}{u_n} = 2$

The sequence 1, 5, 13, 29, ... has the recurrence relation $u_{n+1} = 2u_n + 3$
since $u_2 = 2u_1 + 3$
$\quad\quad u_3 = 2u_2 + 3$, etc.

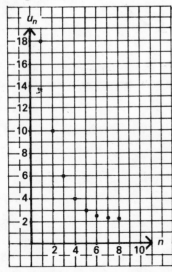

A sequence may tend to a limiting value as $n \to \infty$ (n tends to infinity), e.g. the sequence 18, 10, 6, 4, 3, 2·5, 2·25, 2·125, ... has the recurrence relation $u_{n+1} = \frac{1}{2}u_n + 1$.

Notice that the decimal part after the '2' will tend to zero as n tends to infinity but the 2 will remain intact no matter how many terms of the sequence are taken. The limiting value of this sequence is then 2. A graph for this sequence is shown here.

Algebra

Sequences often arise in problem solving and the following method of approach can assist in finding the nth term, u_n, when simple inspection fails. An alternative method can be found under the section *What's the Difference? An Investigation* on page 82.

Example

Find the n_{th} term, u_n, for the sequence 2, 5, 8, 11, ...

First we pair off the sequence of natural numbers with each term, i.e.

| sequence | 2 | 5 | 8 | 11 .... u_n |
| natural numbers | 1 | 2 | 3 | 4 .... n |

Now check to see if by multiplying the set of natural numbers by some factor, 2 say, we can come close to the terms of the sequence, i.e.

| sequence | 2 | 5 | 8 | 11 .... u_n |
| 2 × natural numbers | 2 | 4 | 6 | 8 .... 2_n |

Now check to see if by adding or subtracting a constant from $2n$ we can come closer to the sequence.

Since this obviously does not satisfy the sequence we will try multiplying the natural numbers by 3, i.e.

| sequence | 2 | 5 | 8 | 11 .... u_n |
| 3 × natural numbers | 3 | 6 | 9 | 12 .... $3n$ |

It now becomes clear that if 1 is subtracted from $3n$ then we have a match for the original sequence so $u_n = 3n - 1$.

Example

Find u_n when $u_1 = 5$, $u_2 = 8$, $u_3 = 13$, $u_4 = 20$.

| sequence | 5 | 8 | 13 | 20 .... u_n |
| natural numbers | 1 | 2 | 3 | 4 .... n |

Since multiplying by 2, 3, 4 does not give a common difference between the sequences we square the natural numbers, i.e.

| sequence | 5 | 8 | 13 | 20 .... u_n |
| (natural numbers)^2 | 1 | 4 | 9 | 16 .... n^2 |

Clearly we must add 4 to each term of the sequence n^2 thus $u_n = n^2 + 4$.

Note that if squaring the sequence of natural numbers fails to give a common difference between the sequences then we could try cubing the natural numbers.

Algebra

Patterns give rise to sequences as can be seen from the following problems.

Example

If each side of the small squares needs one matchstick how many matchsticks will be required to make the nth pattern of the sequence?

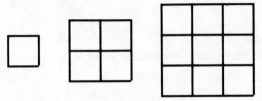

Always start with the simplest pattern and examine its structure. Here each pattern consists of rows and columns of matchsticks.

The first	pattern has	2 rows and	2 columns.
The second	pattern has	3 rows and	3 columns.
The third	pattern has	4 rows and	4 columns.
The nth	pattern has	$(n + 1)$ rows and	$(n + 1)$ columns.

Now in each row and each column there are n matchsticks so the nth pattern requires $n(n + 1) + n(n + 1) = 2n(n + 1)$ matchsticks.

Example

How many dots will be required to make the nth pattern of the sequence?

Here each pattern after the first has four arms of dots and a dot in the centre.

The first	pattern has	(4×0)	+ 1 dot.
The second	pattern has	(4×1)	+ 1 dot.
The third	pattern has	(4×2)	+ 1 dot.
The nth	pattern has	$(4 \times (n - 1))$	+ 1 dot.

The number of dots required for the nth pattern is the $4n - 3$.

8

POLYNOMIALS AND THE REMAINDER THEOREM

$2x^4 + x^3 - 3x^2 + 4x - 5$ is a polynomial of degree 4 because the highest power of x is 4, all the powers of x are elements of W and all the coefficients of the terms are not zero. Since the only variable used is 'x' then this is a polynomial in x.

$5x^3 + 2x^2 + 4$ and $ax^3 + bx^2 + c$ are both polynomials in x of degree 3. These two polynomials are equal when $a = 5$, $b = 2$ and $c = 4$.

The value of a polynomial is found by substitution, e.g. the value of $5x^3 + 2x^2 + 4$ when $x = 2$ is

$$5(2)^3 + 2(2)^2 + 4 = 40 + 8 + 4 = 52.$$

When using a calculator to evaluate a polynomial it is useful to use 'nesting', i.e.

$$(((5x + 2)x + 0)x + 4) = (((10 + 2)2 + 0)2 + 4) = 52.$$

Notice that a zero is inserted to fill the gap due to the absence of any term in x.

The above method can again be simplified for such evaluation by writing down only the coefficients of the variable in descending order of the degree of the variable, e.g.

2	5	2	0	4	⇔		5	2	0	4
		5.2	12.2	24.2				10	24	48
	5	12	24	52			5	12	24	52

If the value of x in the general polynomial of degree 3, $ax^3 + bx^2 + cx + d$, is replaced by h then the value is calculated in the same way, i.e.

h	a	b	c	d
		ah	$ah^2 + bh$	$ah^3 + bh^2 + ch$
	a	$ah + b$	$ah^2 + bh + c$	$ah^3 + bh^2 + ch + d$

The value of the polynomial is the $ah^3 + bh^2 + ch + d$.

The equation $(x - 2)(5x + 2) = 0$ is true when x is replaced by 2. This equation may be written in a more recognisable polynomial form as $5x^2 - 8x - 4 = 0$ and by using the above method

2	5	–8	–4
		10	4
	5	2	0

Notice that the bottom line contains the coefficient of x and the constant from the second bracket of the equation, i.e. the '5' and the '2'.

Algebra

Notice also that the third number in the bottom line is '0'.

This tells us that when $x - 2$ is a factor of the polynomial then the third line will give the coefficients of the remaining factor, $(5x + 2)$. It only remains to discover the significance of the '0'.

In fact the '0' indicates that there is no remainder when the polynomial is divided by $x - 2$.

For example $\dfrac{5x - 8x - 1}{x - 2}$ may be treated by long division as follows:

$$
\begin{array}{r}
5x + 2 \\
x - 2 \overline{\smash{\big)}\ 5x^2 - 8x - 1} \\
\underline{5x^2 - 10x} \\
2x - 1 \\
\underline{2x - 4} \\
\text{Remainder} = 3
\end{array}
\qquad \text{OR} \qquad
\begin{array}{r|rrr}
2 & 5 & -8 & -1 \\
  &   & 10 & 4 \\
\hline
  & 5 & 2 & \underline{3} = \text{Remainder}
\end{array}
$$

i.e. $5x^2 - 8x - 1 = (x - 2)(5x + 2) + 3$.

In general a polynomial $f(x) = (x - h)(Q(x)) + R$.

By using the above method we can say three things

1. when $R = 0$ then $x - h$ is a factor of the polynomial,
2. when $R \neq 0$ then R represents the remainder on division of the polynomial by $x - h$,
3. R represents the value of the polynomial when x is replaced by h.

Examples

(a) Find the factors of $3x^3 + 4x^2 - 13x + 6$.

$$
\begin{array}{r|rrrr}
h = 1 & 3 & 4 & -13 & 6 \\
       &   & 3 & 7 & -6 \\
\hline
h = -3 & 3 & 7 & -6 & \underline{0} \\
       &   & -9 & 6 & \\
\hline
       & 3 & -2 & \underline{0} &
\end{array}
$$

$\Leftrightarrow \quad (x - 1)$ is a factor

$\Leftrightarrow \quad (x + 3)$ is a factor and $(3x - 2)$ is a factor.

Thus $3x^3 + 4x^2 - 13x + 6 \Leftrightarrow (x - 1)(x + 3)(3x - 2)$.

Notice how the above example makes use of the first quotient $3x^2 + 7x - 6$ to find the next factor.

(b) Find the remainder on division of $3x^3 + 4x^2 - 13x + 7$ by $x - 1$.

$$
\begin{array}{r|rrrr}
1 & 3 & 4 & -13 & 7 \\
  &   & 3 & 7 & -6 \\
\hline
  & 3 & 7 & -6 & \underline{1} \;\; = R
\end{array}
$$

Remainder = 1

(c) Evaluate $f(-3)$ when $f(x) = 3x^3 + 4x^2 - 13x + 8$

$$
\begin{array}{r|rrrr}
-3 & 3 & 4 & -13 & 8 \\
   &   & -9 & 15 & -6 \\
\hline
   & 3 & -5 & 2 & \underline{2} \;\; = \;\; f(-3)
\end{array}
$$

(d) Find the value of k for which $x^3 - 3x^2 + kx + 6$ has a factor $(x + 3)$.

$$
\begin{array}{r|rrrr}
-3 & 1 & -3 & k & 6 \\
   &   & -3 & 18 & -3k-54 \\
\hline
   & 1 & -6 & 18+k & -3k-48 \;\; = R
\end{array}
$$

If $(x + 3)$ is a factor then $R = -3k - 48 = 0$

$$\Leftrightarrow \quad 3k = -48$$
$$\Leftrightarrow \quad k = -16$$

(e) Show that $(3x - 2)$ is a factor of $3x^3 + 4x^2 - 13x + 6$. First change $(3x - 2)$ to the form $3(x - \tfrac{2}{3})$. Now show that $(x - \tfrac{2}{3})$ is a factor.

$$
\begin{array}{r|rrrr}
\tfrac{2}{3} & 3 & 4 & -13 & 6 \\
   &   & 2 & 4 & -6 \\
\hline
   & 3 & 6 & -9 & \underline{0} \;\;\Leftrightarrow\;\; (x - \tfrac{2}{3}) \text{ is a factor.}
\end{array}
$$

Now $3x^3 + 4x^2 - 13x + 6 = (x - \tfrac{2}{3})(3x^2 + 6x - 9)$.

If we now multiply the first factor by 3 giving $(3x - 2)$ we must divide the second factor by 3 giving $(x^2 + 2x - 3)$, thus the factors are
$(3x - 2)(x^2 + 2x - 3) \quad \Leftrightarrow \quad (3x - 2)(x - 1)(x + 3)$.

Algebra

QUADRATIC EQUATIONS AND FUNCTIONS

$ax^2 + bx + c$ is a quadratic expression.

$ax^2 + bx + c = 0$ is a quadratic equation.

If a, b, c are real then the expression and the equation are said to be real.

If a, b, c are rational then the expression and the equation are said to be rational.

Although the coefficients of an equation are real and rational the roots (the solution set) need not be so.

The nature of the roots is determined by using the discriminant, i.e. $b^2 - 4ac$, which comes from the formula for finding the roots of a quadratic equation, i.e.

$$x = \frac{-b \pm \sqrt{b^2 - 4ac}}{2a}$$

1. If $b^2 - 4ac = 0$ the roots are $\dfrac{-b + 0}{2a}$ and $\dfrac{-b - 0}{2a}$ i.e. both roots are co-incident

    at $\dfrac{-b}{2a}$. Such a condition arises when the graph of the function is as in the figure below.

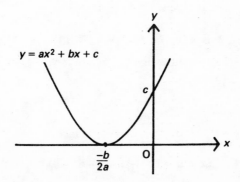

In this figure the roots are shown to be identical when the x-axis is a tangent at the point on the curve where $x = \dfrac{-b}{2a}$, assuming a, $b > 0$.

The nature of the roots depends on the nature of $\dfrac{-b}{2a}$ and the equation or expression will be of the same nature.

12

2. If $b^2 - 4ac > 0$ the roots are $\dfrac{-b + \sqrt{b^2 - 4ac}}{2a}$ and $\dfrac{-b - \sqrt{b^2 - 4ac}}{2a}$.

Such a condition arises when the graph of the function is as in the figure below.

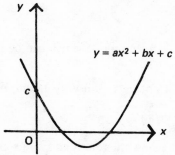

In this figure the roots are the values of x where the curve cuts the x-axis, assuming both roots are positive.

3. If $b^2 - 4ac < 0$ then the roots do not belong to the set of real numbers, since the root of a negative number, i.e. $b^2 - 4ac < 0$ is not a real number. Such a condition arises when the graph of the function is as in the figure below.

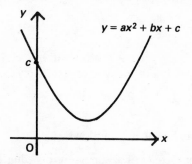

In this figure the graph does not cut the x-axis and so the equation it represents has no real roots. By testing the discriminant, $b^2 - 4ac$, the nature of the factors of $f(x) = ax^2 + bx + c$ are determined. When the condition illustrated in 3 above arises we say the expression is irreducible, i.e. when no real factors exist.

All the diagrams shown have assumed that 'a', the coefficient of x^2, is positive. If 'a' is negative then the graphs of the functions will have maximum turning values and the graphs would appear reflected in the x-axis but all the information gathered would stand as before.

Algebra

COMPLETING THE SQUARE

The method of completing the square may be used with
1. quadratic functions
2. quadratic equations.

1. $f(x) = 2x^2 - 3x - 5$ is a function of x which can be reformed by completing the square as follows.

   (i) Make the coefficient of x^2 unity by taking out a factor of 2 giving
   $$f(x) = 2\left(x^2 - \frac{3}{2}x - \frac{5}{2} \right).$$

   (ii) Go inside the brackets then both add and subtract the square of half the coefficient of x giving
   $$f(x) = 2\left(x^2 - \frac{3}{2}x + \frac{9}{16} - \frac{5}{2} - \frac{9}{16} \right)$$

   (iii) Rearrange the terms inside the brackets giving
   $$f(x) = 2\left(\left[(x - \tfrac{3}{4})^2 \right] - \frac{49}{16} \right)$$
   $$= 2(x - \tfrac{3}{4})^2 - \frac{49}{8}$$

   The above form of $f(x)$ provides information useful in sketching the graph of $f(x)$, e.g. the equation of the axis of symmetry is $x = \tfrac{3}{4}$ and the minimum value of $f(x)$ is $-\frac{49}{8}$.

2. $2x^2 - 3x - 5 = 0$ may be solved as follows.

   (i) Make the coefficient of x^2 unity by dividing throughout by 2 giving
   $$x^2 - \frac{3}{2}x - \frac{5}{2} = 0.$$

   (ii) Take the constant to the right hand side of the equation giving
   $$x^2 - \frac{3}{2}x = \frac{5}{2}$$

   (iii) Square half the coefficient of x and add the result to both sides of the equation giving $x^2 - \frac{3}{2}x + \frac{9}{16} = \frac{5}{2} + \frac{9}{16}$

14

(iv) Rearrange the left hand side of the equation thus

$$(x - \tfrac{3}{4})^2 = \frac{49}{16}$$

(v) Take the square root of both sides of the equation giving

$$x - \tfrac{3}{4} = \pm \frac{7}{4}$$

$$\Leftrightarrow x = \frac{5}{2} \text{ or } -1$$

The method of completing the square can be used to derive the formula for the solution of the general quadratic equation $ax^2 + bx + c = 0$.

$$ax^2 + bx + c = 0$$

$\Rightarrow x^2 + \dfrac{b}{a}x + \dfrac{c}{a} = 0$ (i.e. by dividing throughout by a)

$\Rightarrow x^2 + \dfrac{b}{a}x \qquad = -\dfrac{c}{a}$ (i.e. taking constant to the right hand side of the equation)

$\Rightarrow x^2 + \dfrac{b}{a}x + \dfrac{b^2}{4a^2} = \dfrac{b^2}{4a^2} - \dfrac{c}{a}$ (i.e. adding square of half the coefficient of x to both sides of the equation)

$\Rightarrow \left(x + \dfrac{b}{2a}\right)^2 = \dfrac{b^2}{4a^2} - \dfrac{4ac}{4a^2}$ $\left(\text{i.e. rearranging left hand side and note } \dfrac{c}{a} = \dfrac{4ac}{4a^2}\right)$

$$= \dfrac{b^2 - 4ac}{4a^2}$$

$\Rightarrow x + \dfrac{b}{2a} = \pm \sqrt{\dfrac{b^2 - 4ac}{4a^2}}$ (i.e. taking the square root of both sides of the equation)

$$= \pm \dfrac{\sqrt{b^2 - 4ac}}{2a}$$

$$\Rightarrow x \qquad = -\dfrac{b}{2a} \pm \dfrac{\sqrt{b^2 - 4ac}}{2a}$$

$$= \dfrac{-b \pm \sqrt{b^2 - 4ac}}{2a}$$

Algebra

IRRATIONALS

Irrationals of form $p \pm \sqrt{q}$

Because the formula for solving the quadratic equation is of the form

$$x = \frac{-b \pm \sqrt{b^2 - 4ac}}{2a}$$

$$= \frac{-b}{2a} + \frac{\sqrt{b^2 - 4ac}}{2a} \text{ or } \frac{-b}{2a} - \frac{\sqrt{b^2 - 4ac}}{2a}$$

$$= p + \sqrt{q} \text{ or } p - \sqrt{q}$$

then given one root of a quadratic equation it is clear what the other root must be. For example if $2 + \sqrt{3}$ is a root of a quadratic equation then $2 - \sqrt{3}$ is the other root.

Irrational numbers which differ only in the sign between the first and second terms are called conjugates of each other.

Thus $2 + \sqrt{3}$ is the conjugate of $2 - \sqrt{3}$ and vice versa.

Rationalising the denominator $p \pm \sqrt{q}$

The evaluation of the form $\dfrac{r}{p + \sqrt{q}}$ or $\dfrac{r}{p - \sqrt{q}}$ can be awkward, but the following method simplifies the working.

Example

Evaluate $\dfrac{7}{3 - \sqrt{2}}$ correct to 3 decimal places.

First find the conjugate of the denominator, i.e. $3 + \sqrt{2}$. Now multiply the numerator and the denominator by it, i.e.

$$\frac{7}{3 - \sqrt{2}} \frac{3 + \sqrt{2}}{3 + \sqrt{2}} = \frac{7(3 + \sqrt{2})}{9 - 2}$$

$$= \frac{7(3 + \sqrt{2})}{7}$$

$$= 3 + \sqrt{2}$$

$$= 3 + 1{\cdot}414$$

$$= 4{\cdot}414 \text{ to 3 d.p's}$$

Note that conjugate surds are of the form $a + b$, and $a - b$ so their product is $(a + b)(a - b) = a^2 - b^2$ thus $(3 - \sqrt{2})(3 + \sqrt{2}) = 3^2 - (\sqrt{2})^2 = 9 - 2 = 7$.

FUNCTIONS

A function is a mapping of the set A, called the domain, on to a set B, called the range, such that for every element in A there is one and only one corresponding image in B. In symbols, if $a \in A$ then $f(a) \in B$.

When only a few elements are involved in each set the function or mapping may be represented by a list of ordered pairs where the first member is from the set A and the second member is from the set B. If A = {1, 2, 3, 4} and the rule 'f' means 'multiply the element of A by 2 to find $f(a)$' then the ordered pairs are (1, 2), (2, 4), (3, 6), (4, 8). This can be represented in an arrow diagram as shown

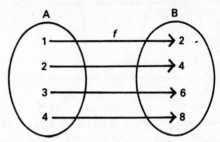

or in a cartesian diagram as follows.

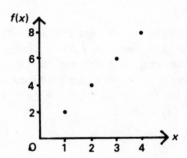

Notice that each and every element in the domain, A, must have an image in the set B, but not all of the elements in B need to be images, e.g.

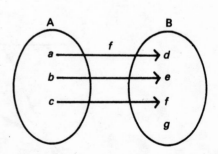

The set B is called the codomain, i.e. {d, e, f, g} and the subset {d, e, f} is called the range.

Algebra

When every element of B is an image then a one-to-one correspondence is established and gives rise to an inverse function, i.e. a mapping of the set B on to the set A. This inverse function is denoted by the symbol f^{-1}. The following diagrams illustrate the inverse of a function.

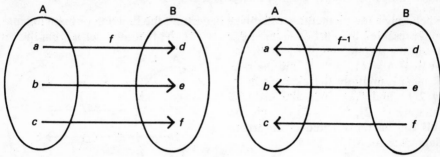

Notice that when a function has an inverse then the domain, A becomes the range and the range B becomes the domain for f^{-1}.

The inverse of a function is also a function and must obey the rules of a function.

The graphs of a function and its inverse are illustrated here. Notice that the graph of the inverse of a function is its image under a reflection in the line $y = x$. Here $f(x) = 2x + 4$ and $f^{-1}(x) = \frac{1}{2}x - 2$

$f(x) = 2x + 4$

$f(x) = x$

$f^{-1}(x) = \frac{1}{2}x - 2$

Having mapped a set A on to a set B there is no reason why we should not extend the process and so map the set B on to a set C.

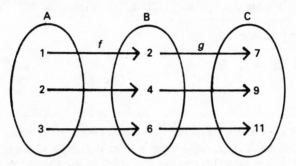

Here 'f' means 'multiply each element of A by 2', and 'g' means 'add 5 to each element of B'.

By omitting the middle step we could describe a function or mapping h which maps the set A on to the set C.

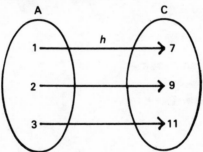

Here $h(x) = 2x + 5$ or $h(x) = g(f(x))$.

Note that the order is the same as the original steps, i.e. f first then g, which means multiply x by 2 then add 5 to the result.

What we are doing here is taking the range of A, which is B, and then using the set B as a domain from which we establish a new range, namely the set C.

The function h which goes from set A to set C is a composite of g and f.

In general if f and g are functions with domains A (for f) and B (for g) then the composition of functions $g(f(x))$ is a new function, $h(x)$ where the domain of $h(x) = \{x : x \in A, f(x) \in B\}$.

Algebra

THE LAWS OF LOGARITHMS

$\text{Log } pq = \log p + \log q$

$\text{Log } \dfrac{p}{q} = \log p - \log q$

$\text{Log } p^n = n \log p$

$\text{Log}_a a = 1$

$\text{Log}_a 1 = 0$

The two most commonly used bases for logarithms are 10 and e ($2 \cdot 72$ to 2 d.p.). When the base used is obvious then it does not have to be indicated in the notation, e.g. if it is clear that the base e is being used then $\log x$ is acceptable notation. It should be noted that $\log_e x$ is sometimes printed as lnx as on many calculators.

Examples

(a) Find x when $\log_x 49 = 2$

$\quad \log_x 49 = 2$

$\Leftrightarrow x^2 = 49$

$\Leftrightarrow x = 7 \quad$ (Remember $x > 0$)

(b) Find x when $\log_{\frac{1}{4}} 64 = x$

$\quad \log_{\frac{1}{4}} 64 = x$

$\Leftrightarrow (\frac{1}{4})^x = 64$

$\Leftrightarrow (\frac{1}{4})^x = 4^3$

$\Leftrightarrow (\frac{1}{4})^x = (\frac{1}{4})^{-3}$

$\Leftrightarrow x = -3$

(c) Solve $\log_5 (3 - 2x) + \log_5 (2 + x) = 1, x \in R$.

$\quad \log_5 (3 - 2x) + \log_5 (2 + x) = \log_5 (3 - 2x)(2 + x)$
$\quad\quad\quad\quad\quad\quad\quad\quad\quad\quad\quad\quad\quad\quad = \log_5 (6 - x - 2x^2)$

$\Leftrightarrow \log_5 (6 - x - 2x^2) = 1$

$\Leftrightarrow 6 - x - 2x^2 = 5^1$

$\Leftrightarrow 2x^2 + x - 1 = 0$

$\Leftrightarrow (2x - 1)(x + 1) = 0$

$\Leftrightarrow x = \frac{1}{2} \quad\quad x = -1$

The base e is useful in calculations involving natural growth or decay as occurs in plants or radioactive elements. This law is of the form $A_t = A_o\, e^{kt}$ where A_o stands for a value at a chosen origin in time and A_t *for the value at another time,* e is the constant 2·72, t again is the other time and k a constant, positive for growth, negative for decay.

Example

A radioactive element decays at a rate given by $M_t = M_o e^{-kt}$ where M_o is the initial mass and M_t is the mass after t years. If $M_o = 50$ gm find the half life of the element given $k = 0.05$. The half life occurs when the mass is half the original, i.e. when $M_t = \frac{1}{2}M_o$.

$$M_t = M_o e^{-0.05t}$$

$$\tfrac{1}{2}M_o = M_o e^{-0.05t}$$

$$\tfrac{1}{2} = e^{-0.05t}$$

$$\log 0.5 = \log(e^{-0.05t})$$

$$\log 0.5 = -0.05t \log e$$

$$t = \frac{\log 0.5}{-0.05 \log e} \qquad \text{(note how convenient base } e \text{ would be here}$$
$$\text{since } \log_e e = 1)$$

$$t = 13.9 \text{ to 3 s.f.}$$

The half life is then after 13·9 years.

Algebra

GRAPHS OF EXPONENTIAL AND LOGARITHMIC FUNCTIONS

If $x = e^y$ then by the laws of logarithms

$\log x = \log e^y$ (using logs to base e)

$\quad\quad = y \log e$

$\quad\quad = y$

i.e. $y = \log x$

The logarithmic function then is the inverse of the exponential function.

The graphs of e^x and $\log x$ are reflections of each other in the line $y = x$.

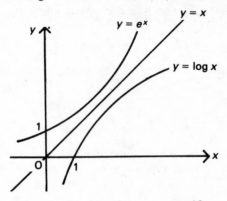

Compare the above graph with that given on page 18.

Though the above has used the base e the same would hold for any base a, $a > 0$, $a \neq 1$ and $x \in R$. The inverse of $f(x) = a^x$ is $f^{-1}(x) = \log_a x$.

The graphs of e^x and e^{-x} are shown below.

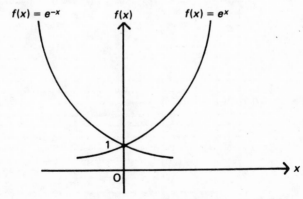

THE FORM $y = ax^n$

If x and y are two variables connected by the law $y = ax^n$ then by the laws of logs.

$$\log y = \log a + \log x^n$$
$$= \log a + n \log x$$
$$= n \log x + \log a$$

By substitution $Y = \log y$, $X = \log x$ and $c = \log a$ the above equation may be written in the form $Y = nX + c$ which is the form of an equation of a straight line.

In general the graph of $\log y$ against $\log x$ is a straight line $\Leftrightarrow y = ax^n$.

Example

Corresponding readings of x and y in an experiment are given in the table.

x	2·0	2·5	3·0	4·0	5·0
y	0·8	1·25	1·8	3·2	5·0

Show that $y = ax^n$ and find the value of a and of n.

Using logs the table is converted to

$\log x$	0·30	0·40	0·48	0·60	0·70
$\log y$	−0·10	0·10	0·26	0·51	0·70

(logs to base 10)

Plotting $\log x$ against $\log y$ and drawing the best fitting straight line gives the diagram below.

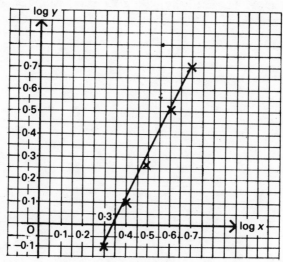

Algebra

Choosing the points $(0.4, 0.10)$ and $(0.70, 0.70)$ from the graph gives

$$n = \frac{0.70 - 0.10}{0.70 - 0.40} = \frac{0.6}{0.3} = 2$$

$c = \log a$ so by substitution in $\log y = n \log x + \log a$ we find

$$0.70 = 2(0.7) + \log a$$
$$\log a = -0.7$$
$$a = 0.20 \text{ to 2 significant figures}$$

Thus the law connecting x and y is $y = 0.20 x^2$

VECTORS

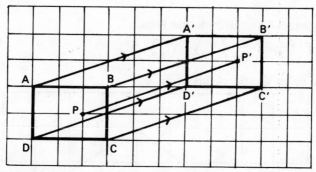

If rectangle ABCD is moved or translated to position A′B′C′D′ then it will have been translated 6 units to the right and 2 units up. This translation can be represented by a vector, $\underline{v}$. The '6' and the '2' are called the components of the vector $\underline{v}$ and is written $\underline{v} = \begin{pmatrix} 6 \\ 2 \end{pmatrix}$.

Since every point on ABCD has been moved to a corresponding point on A′B′C′D′ then $\underline{v} = \{ \overrightarrow{AA'}, \overrightarrow{BB'}, \ldots\ldots \overrightarrow{PP'}, \ldots\ldots \overrightarrow{CC'}, \overrightarrow{DD'} \}$. The elements in this set are called directed line segments and are indicated in the above diagram by the arrowed lines. Notice that all the directed line segments are equal in length or magnitude, they are all parallel, i.e. have the same direction and are all going from ABCD to A′B′C′D′, i.e. all have the same sense.

Vectors which have the same magnitude, direction and sense are said to be equal. If $\underline{v} = \underline{u}$ and $\underline{u} = \begin{pmatrix} a \\ b \end{pmatrix}$ then $a = 6$ and $b = 2$.

The length or magnitude of a vector (written $| \underline{v} |$) is found by considering the directed line segment which represents the vector as the hypotenuse of a right-angled triangle and using the theorem of Pythagoras, i.e. $| \underline{v} | = \sqrt{6^2 + 2^2}$.

If $\underline{v} = k\underline{u}$, k is a constant, then the vectors $\underline{v}$ and $\underline{u}$ are parallel, i.e. have the same direction but they are different in magnitude, e.g. if $k = 2$ then $\underline{v} = \begin{pmatrix} 6 \\ 2 \end{pmatrix} = 2 \begin{pmatrix} 3 \\ 1 \end{pmatrix}$ and so $\underline{u} = \begin{pmatrix} 3 \\ 1 \end{pmatrix}$. If $k = \pm 1$ the $\underline{u}$ and $\underline{v}$ have the same magnitude. If k is positive the vectors have the same sense but if k is negative then the vectors have opposite sense, e.g. from the diagram above $\overrightarrow{AA'} = -\overrightarrow{A'A}$, i.e. $\begin{pmatrix} 6 \\ 2 \end{pmatrix} = -1 \begin{pmatrix} -6 \\ -2 \end{pmatrix}$.

Geometry

ADDITION OF VECTORS

Vectors may be added to give another vector,

e.g. $\begin{pmatrix} 4 \\ 3 \end{pmatrix} + \begin{pmatrix} 3 \\ -2 \end{pmatrix} = \begin{pmatrix} 4+3 \\ 3+(-2) \end{pmatrix} = \begin{pmatrix} 7 \\ 1 \end{pmatrix}$.

The diagram below illustrates this addition.

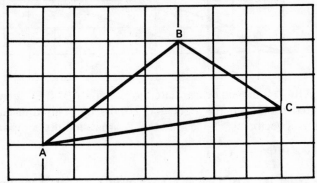

Here $\overrightarrow{AB} + \overrightarrow{BC} = \overrightarrow{AC}$, i.e. to go from A to C is the same vector as in going from A to B and then from B to C.

To go from B to C is the same vector as in going from B to A and then from A to C, i.e. $\overrightarrow{BC} = \overrightarrow{BA} + \overrightarrow{AC}$ or $\overrightarrow{BC} = \overrightarrow{AC} - \overrightarrow{AB}$ since $\overrightarrow{BA} = -\overrightarrow{AB}$.

POSITION VECTORS

So far all the vectors have been free vectors, i.e. they have not been referenced to any origin. It is often convenient to work with reference to an origin and such vectors are called position vectors.

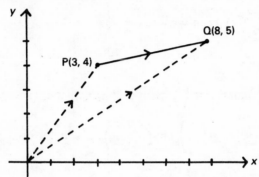

If P(3, 4) and Q(8, 5) as in the diagram then $\overrightarrow{OP} = \begin{pmatrix} 3 \\ 4 \end{pmatrix}$ and $\overrightarrow{OQ} = \begin{pmatrix} 8 \\ 5 \end{pmatrix}$, with reference to the origin, and $\overrightarrow{PQ}$ can be expressed in component form

$$\overrightarrow{PQ} = \overrightarrow{OQ} - \overrightarrow{OP}$$
$$= \begin{pmatrix} 8 \\ 5 \end{pmatrix} - \begin{pmatrix} 3 \\ 4 \end{pmatrix}$$
$$= \begin{pmatrix} 5 \\ 1 \end{pmatrix}$$

$\overrightarrow{OP}$ may be written as $3i + 4j$ where i is a unit vector, i.e. a vector of magnitude equal to 1 which is parallel to the x-axis and j a unit vector parallel to the y-axis. Similarly $\overrightarrow{OQ} = 8i + 5j$. $\overrightarrow{PQ}$ then is $5i + j$. i and j are called basis vectors and any three vectors of the form $xi + yj$ are said to be linearly dependent, i.e. any one of them can be expressed as a combination of the other two.

Geometry

Example

Express $2i + 3j$ as a combination of $i + j$ and $3i - 2j$.

Let $2i + 3j = x(i + j) + y(3i - 2j)$
$\qquad\qquad = (x + 3y)i + (x - 2y)j$

Thus $\quad \left.\begin{array}{l} 2 = x + 3y \\ 3 = x - 2y \end{array}\right\} \Leftrightarrow -1 = 5y \Leftrightarrow y = -\dfrac{1}{5}$

$$x = \frac{13}{5}$$

Note that $i = \begin{pmatrix} 1 \\ 0 \end{pmatrix}$ and $j = \begin{pmatrix} 0 \\ 1 \end{pmatrix}$ when dealing with 2 dimensional vectors but in

3 dimensional vectors $i = \begin{pmatrix} 1 \\ 0 \\ 0 \end{pmatrix}$ and $j = \begin{pmatrix} 0 \\ 1 \\ 0 \end{pmatrix}$. k will be used as a unit vector

parallel to the z-axis and $k = \begin{pmatrix} 0 \\ 0 \\ 1 \end{pmatrix}$.

SPACE DIAGONALS

Figure 1

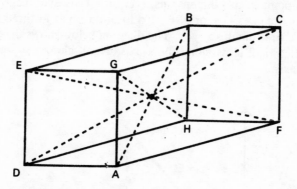

Figure 1 shows a cuboid with its 4 space diagonals. AB = CD = EF = GH. The lengths of these space diagonals can be calculated by using the theorem of Pythagoras twice over.

Figure 2

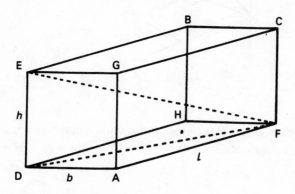

In figure 2 triangles EDF and ADF are right-angled.

$DF^2 = l^2 + b^2$

$EF^2 = DF^2 + h^2$

$\quad = l^2 + b^2 + h^2$

$EF \ = \sqrt{l^2 + b^2 + h^2}$

DF is called a face diagonal, and DG is another face diagonal. Note that face diagonals are not equal unless $l = b = h$, i.e. when the figure is a cube.

Geometry

3D CO-ORDINATES

To locate a point in two dimensions, e.g. on a Cartesian diagram, we require two co-ordinates, i.e. x, y or r, $\theta°$. To locate a point in three dimensions we require three co-ordinates x, y, z. The diagram below shows the point $P(x, y, z)$ i.e. (2, 1, 4). P is 2 units along the x-axis, 1 unit along the y-axis and 4 units along the z-axis.

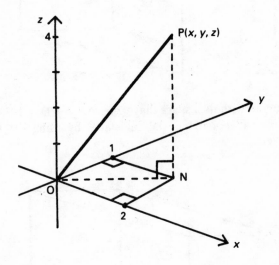

Note that the distance OP is found by the same method as was used to find the length of space diagonals, i.e. $OP = \sqrt{x^2 + y^2 + z^2} = \sqrt{2^2 + 1^2 + 4^2} = \sqrt{21}$.

3D VECTORS

If A(2, 3, 4) and B(5, 7, 9) the $\overrightarrow{AB} = \begin{pmatrix} 5-2 \\ 7-3 \\ 9-4 \end{pmatrix} = \begin{pmatrix} 3 \\ 4 \\ 5 \end{pmatrix}$ and $| \overrightarrow{AB} | = \sqrt{3^2 + 4^2 + 5^2}$

Using basis vectors
$\overrightarrow{OA} = 2\underline{i} + 3\underline{j} + 4\underline{k}$, $\overrightarrow{OB} = 5\underline{i} + 7\underline{j} + 9\underline{k}$ and $\overrightarrow{AB} = 3\underline{i} + 4\underline{j} + 5\underline{k}$ where $\underline{k}$ is a unit vector parallel to the z-axis.

To show that two line segments are parallel in two dimensions it is sufficient to show that the two line segments may be represented by linear equations with the same gradient, e.g. $y = mx + c_1$ and $y = mx + c_2$ are parallel because they both have the same gradient m, as in $y = 3x + 5$ and $y = 3x - 9$.

Example

Show that the line segments AB and CD are parallel where A(3, 4), B(5, 7) and C(8, −3) and D(12, 3).

Since only the gradients matter:

$$m_{AB} = \frac{y_B - y_A}{x_B - x_A} \qquad\qquad m_{CD} = \frac{y_D - y_C}{x_D - x_C}$$

$$= \frac{7-4}{5-3} \qquad\qquad\qquad = \frac{3+3}{12-8}$$

$$= \frac{3}{2} \qquad\qquad\qquad\qquad = \frac{6}{4}$$

$$\qquad\qquad\qquad\qquad\qquad = \frac{3}{2}$$

Thus $m_{AB} = m_{CD}$ and so the line segment AB and CD are parallel.

However in three dimensions we do not have a formula corresponding to $\frac{y_2 - y_1}{x_2 - x_1}$ but we have a vector equation to assist in the proof, i.e. $\underline{u} = k\underline{v} \Leftrightarrow \underline{u}$ is parallel to $\underline{v}$.

Geometry

Example

Show that the line segments AB and CD are parallel where A(3, 4, 5), B(5, 7, 9) and C(2, –3, 4) and D(6, 3, 12).

$$\text{Now } \overrightarrow{AB} = \begin{pmatrix} 5-3 \\ 7-4 \\ 9-5 \end{pmatrix} \qquad\qquad \overrightarrow{CD} = \begin{pmatrix} 6-2 \\ 3+3 \\ 12-4 \end{pmatrix}$$

$$= \begin{pmatrix} 2 \\ 3 \\ 4 \end{pmatrix} \qquad\qquad\qquad = \begin{pmatrix} 4 \\ 6 \\ 8 \end{pmatrix}$$

$$= 2\begin{pmatrix} 2 \\ 3 \\ 4 \end{pmatrix}$$

If we now consider $\overrightarrow{AB}$ to be a representative of $\underline{u}$ and $\overrightarrow{CD}$ a representative of $\underline{v}$ then $\underline{u} = \frac{1}{2}\underline{v}$ so $\overrightarrow{AB} = \frac{1}{2}\overrightarrow{CD} \Leftrightarrow \overrightarrow{AB}$ is parallel to $\overrightarrow{CD}$.

Note that to prove two line segments are collinear, i.e. on the same straight line it is sufficient to prove that they are parallel and that there is a common point on both lines.

Example

Prove that AB and BC are collinear where A(3, 4, 5), B(5, 7, 9), C(9, 13, 17).

$$\overrightarrow{AB} = \begin{pmatrix} 2 \\ 3 \\ 4 \end{pmatrix} \qquad\qquad \overrightarrow{BC} = \begin{pmatrix} 4 \\ 6 \\ 8 \end{pmatrix} = 2\begin{pmatrix} 2 \\ 3 \\ 4 \end{pmatrix}$$

i.e. $\overrightarrow{AB} = \frac{1}{2}\overrightarrow{BC} \Leftrightarrow AB$ is parallel to BC and B is a common point thus AB and BC are collinear.

VECTOR ALGEBRA

It is often convenient in working with vectors to express $\overrightarrow{OA} = \underline{a}$, $\overrightarrow{OB} = \underline{b}$, etc.

Since $\overrightarrow{AB} = \overrightarrow{OB} - \overrightarrow{OA}$ then

$$\overrightarrow{AB} = \underline{b} - \underline{a}$$

The following example illustrates the use of this notation.

Let M be the mid-point of AB.

$$\overrightarrow{AB} = \overrightarrow{OB} - \overrightarrow{OA}$$
$$= \underline{b} - \underline{a}$$
$$\overrightarrow{OM} = \overrightarrow{OA} + \tfrac{1}{2}\overrightarrow{AB}$$
$$= \underline{a} + \tfrac{1}{2}(\underline{b} - \underline{a})$$
$$= \underline{a} + \tfrac{1}{2}\underline{b} - \tfrac{1}{2}\underline{a}$$
$$= \tfrac{1}{2}\underline{a} + \tfrac{1}{2}\underline{b}$$
$$= \tfrac{1}{2}(\underline{a} + \underline{b})$$
$$= \tfrac{1}{2}(\overrightarrow{OA} + \overrightarrow{OB})$$

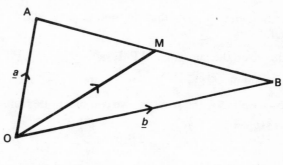

The power of this method is seen in the following example.

Example

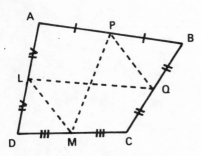

ABCD is a quadrilateral. P and Q are mid-points of AB and BC; L and M are the mid-points of DA and DC. Prove that the mid-points of QL and PM are the same point.

Geometry

Method

First be sure to draw an adequate figure and mark all information given.

Choose an origin, O say, but do not mark it on the diagram for it will render it too complex to be of value.

Change all line segments to position vector notation, .e.g $\overrightarrow{PM}$ becomes $\underline{m} - \underline{p}$, thus we may reduce the geometry problem to one of simple algebra. Now in terms of position vectors list the data given.

$$\underline{p} = \tfrac{1}{2}(\underline{a} + \underline{b}); \quad \underline{q} = \tfrac{1}{2}(\underline{b} + \underline{c}); \quad \underline{l} = \tfrac{1}{2}(\underline{a} + \underline{d}); \quad \underline{m} = \tfrac{1}{2}(\underline{d} + \underline{c})$$

Now we wish to show that the mid-point of PM is the same as the mid-point of QL.

Write down the mid-point of PM, say $\underline{x}_1$

Mid-point of PM, $\underline{x}_1 = \tfrac{1}{2}(\underline{p} + \underline{m})$. Similarly the mid-point of QL, $\underline{x}_2 = \tfrac{1}{2}(\underline{l} + \underline{q})$.

These don't look the same but we can substitute from our given data thus:

$$\underline{x}_1 = \tfrac{1}{2}(\underline{p} + \underline{m}) = \tfrac{1}{2}(\tfrac{1}{2}(\underline{a} + \underline{b}) + \tfrac{1}{2}(\underline{d} + \underline{c}))$$
$$= \tfrac{1}{4}(\underline{a} + \underline{b} + \underline{c} + \underline{d})$$
$$\underline{x}_2 = \tfrac{1}{2}(\underline{l} + \underline{q}) = \tfrac{1}{2}(\tfrac{1}{2}(\underline{a} + \underline{d}) + \tfrac{1}{2}(\underline{b} + \underline{c}))$$
$$= \tfrac{1}{4}(\underline{a} + \underline{b} + \underline{c} + \underline{d})$$
$$= \underline{x}_1$$

Thus the mid-points are the same.

DIVIDING A LINE IN A GIVEN RATIO

If A, B and P are collinear and $\dfrac{AP}{PB} = \dfrac{m}{n}$ then $\overrightarrow{AP} = \dfrac{m}{n}\overrightarrow{PB}$.

A method of finding the point P is illustrated by the following example.

Example

Find the co-ordinates of P which divides AB in the ratio 2 : 3 when A(0, –3, –6) and B(5, 7, 9).

$$
\begin{array}{ccc}
& 2 \qquad\qquad \text{P} \qquad\qquad 3 & \\
\text{A} & \rule{8cm}{0.4pt} & \text{B}
\end{array}
$$

$\overrightarrow{AP} = \frac{2}{5}\overrightarrow{AB}$

$\qquad = \frac{2}{5}\begin{pmatrix} 5 - 0 \\ 7 + 3 \\ 9 + 6 \end{pmatrix}$

$\qquad = \frac{2}{5}\begin{pmatrix} 5 \\ 10 \\ 15 \end{pmatrix}$

$\qquad = \begin{pmatrix} 2 \\ 4 \\ 6 \end{pmatrix}$

But $\overrightarrow{AP} = \overrightarrow{OP} - \overrightarrow{OA}$

so $\overrightarrow{OP} = \overrightarrow{AP} + \overrightarrow{OA}$

$\qquad = \begin{pmatrix} 2 \\ 4 \\ 6 \end{pmatrix} + \begin{pmatrix} 0 \\ -3 \\ -6 \end{pmatrix}$

$\qquad = \begin{pmatrix} 2 \\ 1 \\ 0 \end{pmatrix}$

Thus P is the point (2, 1, 0)

Geometry

In the example on page 35, P is said to divide AB internally since P lies between A and B. If P lies outwith AB then P is said to divide the line externally.

When this is the case, as illustrated below, then the same procedure is used to find P but in the first line the ratio is made negative.

 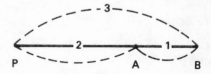

Here $\overrightarrow{AP} = -\frac{2}{3}\overrightarrow{PB}$ and $\overrightarrow{AP} = -\frac{2}{1}\overrightarrow{AB}$

$$= -2\overrightarrow{AB}$$

THE SCALAR PRODUCT

The scalar product of two vectors $\underline{a}$ and $\underline{b}$ is written $\underline{a}.\underline{b}$ where $\underline{a}.\underline{b} = |\underline{a}|\,|\underline{b}|\cos\theta$. θ is the angle between $\underline{a}$ and $\underline{b}$ and lies in the range $0 \leqslant \theta \leqslant \pi$.

If $\underline{a} = \begin{pmatrix} x_1 \\ y_1 \\ z_1 \end{pmatrix}$ and $\underline{b} = \begin{pmatrix} x_2 \\ y_2 \\ z_2 \end{pmatrix}$ then $\underline{a}.\underline{b} = x_1x_2 + y_1y_2 + z_1z_2$.

Notice that although $\underline{a}$ and $\underline{b}$ are vectors $\underline{a}.\underline{b}$ is a scalar (a number).

The angle between two vectors can be found by rearranging the formula

$$\underline{a}.\underline{b} = |\underline{a}|\,|\underline{b}|\cos\theta \text{ giving } \cos\theta = \frac{a.b}{|\underline{a}|\,|\underline{b}|}$$

If $\theta = 90°$ then $\underline{a}.\underline{b} = |\underline{a}|\,|\underline{b}|\cos 90°$.
$$= 0$$

Thus $\underline{a}.\underline{b} = 0$ means that $\underline{a}$ is perpendicular to $\underline{b}$.

Example

Find the size of the angle ABC where A(0, 2, 3), B(−1, 1, 2) and C(−3, 2, 0).

$$\overrightarrow{BA} = \begin{pmatrix} 1 \\ 1 \\ 1 \end{pmatrix} \text{ and } \overrightarrow{BC} = \begin{pmatrix} -2 \\ 1 \\ -2 \end{pmatrix}$$

$$|\overrightarrow{BA}| = \sqrt{3}, |\overrightarrow{BC}| = 3$$

$$\text{Cos } \hat{B} = \frac{-2 + 1 - 2}{3\sqrt{3}}$$

$$= \frac{-1}{\sqrt{3}}$$

$$\hat{B} = 125.3° \text{ to 1 d.p.}$$

Note that the following rule holds in vector scalar multiplication as in the usual algebra:

$$\underline{a}.(\underline{b} + \underline{c}) = \underline{a}.\underline{b} + \underline{a}.\underline{c}$$

Geometry

ALTITUDES, MEDIANS, BISECTORS OF ANGLES AND SIDES, CONCURRENCY

When lines intersect at a common point they are said to be concurrent.

Altitudes, medians, bisectors of angles and sides of a triangle are sets of concurrent lines.

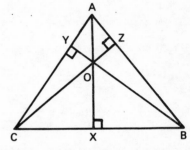

A straight line from a vertex of a triangle perpendicular to the opposite side is called an altitude of the triangle. Every triangle has three altitudes.

In this diagram AX, BY and CZ are the three altitudes of triangle ABC.

The point O is called the orthocentre.

Notice that the three altitudes intersect (cut each other) at the same point.

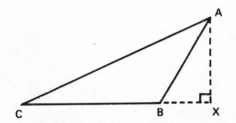

In an obtuse-angled triangle an altitude will lie outside the triangle as in this diagram where AX is an altitude of triangle ABC

A median of a triangle is a straight line from a vertex to the mid-point of the opposite side. Every triangle has three medians.

The diagram shows triangle ABC and a median AM.

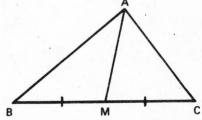

A median divides the triangle into two equal areas. In this diagram the area of triangle ABM = the area of triangle ACM.

38

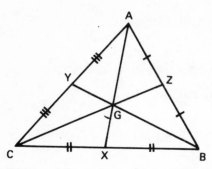

This diagram shows triangle ABC and the three medians AX, BY, CZ.

Notice that the three medians intersect at the same point, G.

The point G is called the centroid of the triangle.

The centroid divides each median in the ratio 2 : 1, i.e. AG = 2GX, BG = 2GY, CG = 2GZ.

If ABC were a setsquare then you could balance it on the point G.

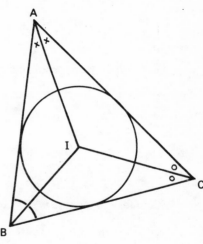

This diagram shows the bisectors of the angles of triangle ABC meeting at the point I, called the incentre, which is the centre of the circle so that each side of the triangle is a tangent to the circle. The circle is said to be inscribed in the triangle.

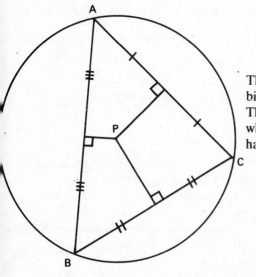

This diagram shows the perpendicular bisectors of the sides of triangle ABC. The circle is called the circumcircle which circumscribes the triangle and has P as centre.

Geometry

THE EQUATION OF A STRAIGHT LINE

There are three main forms of the equation of a straight line.

1. $y = mx + c$ where m is the gradient of the line and c is the value of y where the line cuts the y-axis.

    The gradient m is positive when the angle the line makes with the positive direction of the x-axis is acute.

    The gradient is negative when the angle the line makes with the positive direction of the x-axis is obtuse.

    The gradient is the tangent of the angle the line makes with the positive direction of the x-axis.

    Given two points on the line (x_1, y_1) and (x_2, y_2) then $m = \dfrac{y_2 - y_1}{x_2 - x_1}$, $x_1 \neq x_2$

    Example
    Find the equation of the line passing through A(2, 1) and B(6, 3).
    $$m = \frac{3-1}{6-2}$$
    $$= \tfrac{1}{2}$$
    $$y = \tfrac{1}{2}x + c$$
    Now by substituting one of the points in the equation
    $$1 = \tfrac{1}{2}(2) + c$$
    $c = 0$ (This means the line goes through the origin.)
    The equation of the line is $y = \tfrac{1}{2}x$

2. $y - b = m(x - a)$ where m is the gradient as above and (a, b) a point on the line.

    Example
    Find the equation of the line with gradient 3 passing through (2, 5).
    $$y - 5 = 3(x - 2)$$
    $$y - 5 = 3x - 6$$
    $$y = 3x - 1$$

    This form could be used to solve the example given above by first finding m as above then using one of the given points, i.e.

    $m = \tfrac{1}{2}$ and using A(2, 1) for (a, b) we get
    $$y - 1 = \tfrac{1}{2}(x - 2)$$
    $$\Rightarrow y - 1 = \tfrac{1}{2}x - 1$$
    $$\Rightarrow \quad y = \tfrac{1}{2}x \quad \text{as before.}$$

3. $ax + by + c = 0$ (a, b not both zero)

The gradient can be found by rearranging the equation and dividing by b.

$by = -ax - c$

$y = \dfrac{-a}{b}x - \dfrac{c}{b}$ (compare this equation with $y = mx + c$)

The gradient is $\dfrac{-a}{b}$ and the line cuts the y-axis where $y = \dfrac{-c}{b}$.

Given two lines with equations $y = m_1x + c_1$ and $y = m_2x + c_2$ then they are

1. parallel when $m_1 = m_2$

2. perpendicular when $m_1m_2 = -1$ or $m_1 = \dfrac{-1}{m_2}$.

Example

Find the equation of a line which passes through the point (1, 6) and is *(a)* parallel *(b)* perpendicular to the line $2y - 3x = 5$

(a) By rearranging the equation $2y - 3x = 5$ to $y = \dfrac{3}{2}x + \dfrac{5}{2}$ the gradient of the line parallel to this will be the same, i.e. $\dfrac{3}{2}$ and since (1, 6) lies on the line then by substitution in the form $y - b = m(x - a)$ we get

$y - 6 = \dfrac{3}{2}(x - 1)$

$2y - 12 = 3x - 3$

$2y - 3x = 9$

(b) The gradient of the line perpendicular to one with gradient $\dfrac{3}{2}$ is $-\dfrac{2}{3}$ so by substitution again in the form $y - b = m(x - a)$ we get

$y - 6 = -\dfrac{2}{3}(x - 1)$

$3y - 18 = -2x + 2$

$3y + 2x = 20$

When the gradient $m = 0$ the line is parallel to the x-axis.

When the line is parallel to the x-axis its equation is $y = c$.

When the line is parallel to the y-axis its gradient is undefined and the equation of the line is $x = c$.

Geometry

THE CIRCLE

The equation $x^2 + y^2 = r^2$ describes the locus of a point which is equidistant from the origin, O.

Let $P(x, y)$ be a point on the locus. Then OP is the distance from the origin, i.e. the radius r.

The locus is the set of points $C = \{P(x, y): OP = r\}$.

As is usual with locus problems where the distance formula is involved we square both sides of the equation, thus getting rid of the square root sign in the distance formula, i.e.

$$C = \{P(x, y): OP^2 = r^2\}$$
$$= \{(x, y): (x-0)^2 + (y-0)^2 = r^2\}$$
$$= \{(x, y): x^2 + y^2 = r^2\}$$

Note that $x^2 + y^2 < r^2$ describes the area within the circumference of the circle, and $x^2 + y^2 > r^2$ describes the area outside the circumference of the circle.

If the centre of the circle is taken to be the point $A(a, b)$ then the locus of the points equidistant from A and distance r from it describes the circumference of the circle with centre (a, b) and radius r.

Let $P(x, y)$ be a point on the locus

$$C = \{P(x, y): AP = r\}$$
$$= \{P(x, y): AP^2 = r^2\}$$
$$= \{(x, y): (x-a)^2 + (y-b)^2 = r^2\}$$

By expanding the equation of the circle $(x-a)^2 + (y-b)^2 = r^2$

$$x^2 - 2ax + a^2 + y^2 - 2by + b^2 = r^2$$
$$x^2 + y^2 + 2(-a)x + 2(-b)y + (a^2 + b^2 - r^2) = 0$$
$$x^2 + y^2 + 2(-a)x + 2(-b)y + c = 0$$
$$\text{where } c = (a^2 + b^2 - r^2)$$

Note that the centre has $-(\frac{1}{2}$ the coefficient of $x)$ as its x co-ordinate and $-(\frac{1}{2}$ the coefficient of $y)$ as its y co-ordinate.

In its more general form the equation of a circle is $x^2 + y^2 + 2gx + 2fy + c = 0$.

This form may be proved to represent a circle of centre $(-g, -f)$ and radius $\sqrt{g^2 + f^2 - c}$.

$\{P(x, y) : x^2 + y^2 + 2gx + 2fy + c = 0\}$

$\{P(x, y) : x^2 + 2gx + y^2 + 2fy = -c\}$

Now completing the squares:

$\{P(x, y) : x^2 + 2gx + g^2 + y^2 + 2fy + f^2 = g^2 + f^2 - c^2\}$

$\{P(x, y) : (x + g)^2 + (y + f)^2 = g^2 + f^2 - c\}$

$\{P(x, y) : (x - (-g))^2 + (y - (-f))^2 = g^2 + f^2 - c\}$

$\{P(x, y) : CP^2 = g^2 + f^2 - c\}$

Where C is the point $(-g, -f)$, i.e. the centre of the circle and $\sqrt{g^2 + f^2 - c}$) the distance from the centre to a point $P(x, y)$ on the circumference, i.e. the radius, r.

It is important to note that $g, f, c, \in R$ and that $g^2 + f^2 - c \geqslant 0$ because $g^2 + f^2 - c = r^2 \geqslant 0$.

Geometry

INTERSECTIONS AND QUADRATIC FORMS

A straight line will intersect with a curve whose equation is of quadratic form in

(i)   2 points as in the figure below:

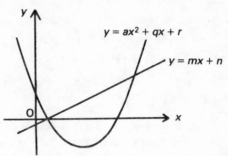

(ii)   1 point, i.e. when the line is a tangent to the curve as in the figure below:

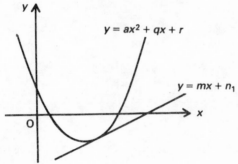

(iii)   or it will not intersect at all as in the figure below:

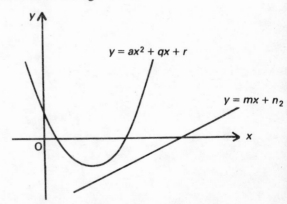

Note that each diagram on page 44 assumes the coefficient of x^2 to be positive though it need not be so.

The intersection between the line and the curve may be found by equating the right-hand sides of the equations of the line and the curve, e.g.

$ax^2 + qx + r = mx + n$

The next step is to solve for x by forming a quadratic equation in its normal form.

$ax^2 + (q-m)x + (r-n) = 0$

i.e. $ax^2 + bx + c \qquad = 0$

$\Leftrightarrow x = \dfrac{-b \pm \sqrt{b^2 - 4ac}}{2a}$

If the discriminant $(b^2 - 4ac) < 0$ then condition (iii) prevails, i.e. there is no solution for $x \in R$.

If the discriminant > 0 then condition (i) prevails, i.e. there are two points of intersection.

If the discriminant $= 0$ then the straight line is a tangent to the curve at that value of x as in condition (ii).

Example

Find the points of intersection between the line $y = 3x + 1$ and the parabola $y = 2x^2 + x - 3$.

$\left.\begin{array}{l} y = 2x^2 + x - 3 \\ y = 3x + 1 \end{array}\right\} \Leftrightarrow 2x^2 + x - 3 = 3x + 1$

$\Leftrightarrow 2x^2 - 2x - 4 = 0$

$\Leftrightarrow x^2 - x - 2 = 0$

$\Leftrightarrow (x - 2)(x + 1) = 0$

$\Leftrightarrow x = 2 \text{ or } x = -1$

By substitution in the equation of the line (or the curve) we can find the corresponding values of y.

i.e. $y = 3(2) + 1 = 7$

$\quad y = 3(-1) + 1 = -2$

i.e. The points of intersection are $(2, 7)$ and $(-1, -2)$.

Geometry

Example

Show that the line $x + y = 3$ is a tangent to the circle $x^2 + y^2 - 6x - 8y + 17 = 0$ and find the coordinates of the point of contact.

In $x^2 + y^2 - 6x - 8y + 17 = 0$ we will substitute $3 - x$ for y giving
$x^2 + (3-x)^2 - 6x - 8(3-x) + 17 = 0$ which when rearranged gives
$2x^2 - 4x + 2 = 0$ which on division throughout by 2 gives $x^2 - 2x + 1 = 0$ which is the same as $(x - 1)^2 = 0$ and has only one solution for x, i.e. $x = 1$. By substitution in $x + y = 3$ gives $y = 2$.

Since there is only one solution then $x + y = 3$ must be a tangent to the given circle at the point $(1, 2)$.

Note that in the equation $x^2 - 2x + 1 = 0$, $b^2 - 4ac = 0$, i.e. the discriminant is zero.

Example

An awkward bend, at X in the diagram, is to be replaced by a gentler parabolic path such that the nearside of each straight stretch of road is a tangent to the parabola at A and B.

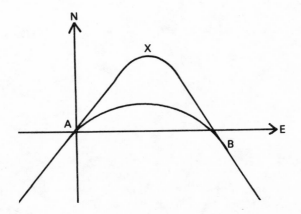

If the section of roadway on which A lies runs S.W. and by taking A as the origin then the section of roadway on which B lies has equation $y = 2 - 3x$. Find the coordinates of B.

46

The equation of road on which A lies is $y = x$ and so has gradient 1, which is the gradient of the tangent to the parabola at A. Similarly the equation of the road on which B lies has equation $y = 2 - 3x$ and so has a gradient -3 which is the gradient of the tangent to the parabola at B.

The gradient of a tangent to the parabola with equation $y = ax^2 + bx + c$ is found by differentiation, thus

$y = ax^2 + bx + c$

$\frac{dy}{dx} = 2ax + b$

giving $1 = b$ at $x = 0$

and $-3 = 2ax + 1$

i.e. $x = \frac{-2}{a}$ at B

and $y = \frac{2}{a}$ at B by substitution, i.e. $B\left(\frac{-2}{a}, \frac{2}{a}\right)$

Since the parabola goes through the origin then $c = 0$ giving the equation $y = ax^2 + x$. We also know that $a < 0$ since the parabola has a maximum turning point.

TRIGONOMETRY

RADIAN MEASURE

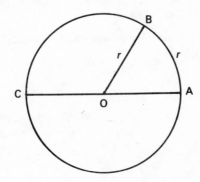

In the diagram the circle with centre O has an arc AB equal in length to the radius, r, of the circle. The circumference of the circle is $2\pi r$.

Arc ABC is half the circumference of the circle and so is of length πr. The length of an arc of the circle, l, depends on the size of the angle, θ, subtended at the centre by the arc, i.e. $l = \dfrac{\theta}{360} \times 2\pi r$.

If we now let $l = r$ then the formula becomes

$$r = \frac{\theta}{360} \times 2\pi r$$

$$= \frac{r\theta\pi}{180}$$

$$\theta = \frac{180}{\pi}$$

Now since both π and 180 are constants then θ must be a constant. This constant, θ, will be given the value of 1 radian, i.e. the size of an angle subtended at the centre of a circle by an arc equal in length to the radius of the circle thus π radians = 180° or simply π = 180°.

It is essential to distinguish between sin $x°$ and sin x where the latter is in radian measure.

Below is an updated version of a familiar table.

Table of exact values of sine, cosine and tangent of certain angles.

	0	$\dfrac{\pi}{6}$	$\dfrac{\pi}{4}$	$\dfrac{\pi}{3}$	$\dfrac{\pi}{2}$
	0°	30°	45°	60°	90°
sin	0	$\dfrac{1}{2}$	$\dfrac{1}{\sqrt{2}}$	$\dfrac{\sqrt{3}}{2}$	1
cos	1	$\dfrac{\sqrt{3}}{2}$	$\dfrac{1}{\sqrt{2}}$	$\dfrac{1}{2}$	0
tan	0	$\dfrac{1}{\sqrt{3}}$	1	$\sqrt{3}$	–

The following should be memorised.

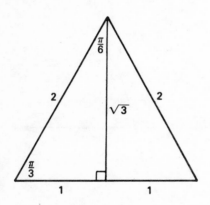

$$\sin A = \sin (\pi - A)$$
$$\cos A = -\cos (\pi - A)$$
$$\tan A = -\tan (\pi - A)$$

$$\sin^2 A + \cos^2 A = 1$$
$$\tan A = \frac{\sin A}{\cos A}$$

Trigonometry

GRAPHS OF SIN x, COS x AND TAN x

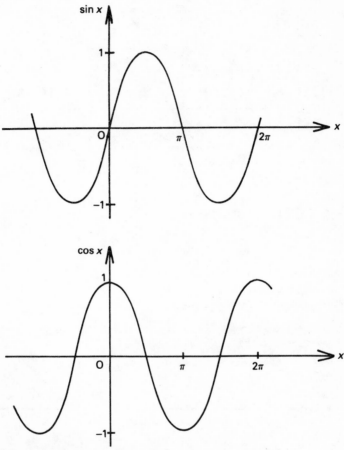

The graph of sin x and cos x repeat the same pattern every 2π.

The *period* of the sine and cosine is 2π.

The maximum value of the sine is 1.

The maximum value of the cosine is 1.

The minimum value of the sine is -1.

The minimum value of the cosine is -1.

The graph of the sine is the same shape as the graph of the cosine when translated $\frac{\pi}{2}$ to the left.

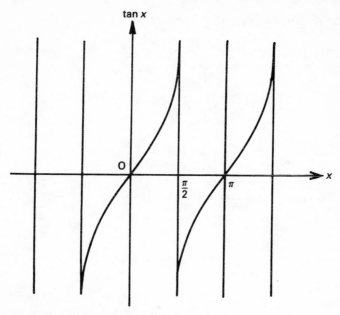

The graph of the tangent repeats its pattern every π.
The period of the tangent is π.
The tangent has no maximum or minimum value.

The following diagram will help to remind you which trigonometric ratios are positive or negative for angles in each quadrant.

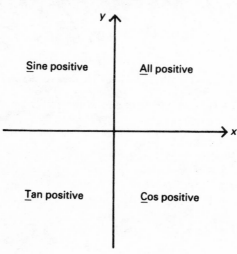

51

Trigonometry

GRAPHS OF SIN 2x, COS 2x, SIN ½x, COS ½x

Note that the period is half
that of sin x.

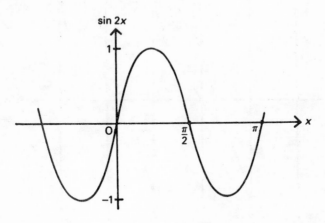

Note that the period is half
that of cos x.

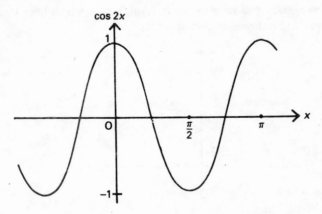

Note that the period is twice
that of sin x.

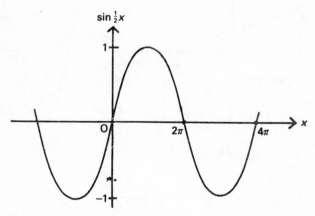

Note that the period is twice
that of cos x.

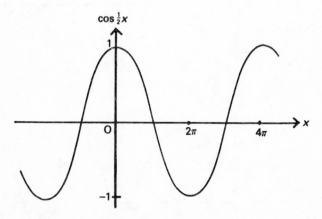

Note that the amplitudes of all the diagrams on the last two pages remain the
same as that of sin x or cos x.

For the sake of comparison the graphs of sin $2x$, sin x and sin $\frac{x}{2}$ are illustrated
on the next page and are drawn to the same scale.

Trigonometry

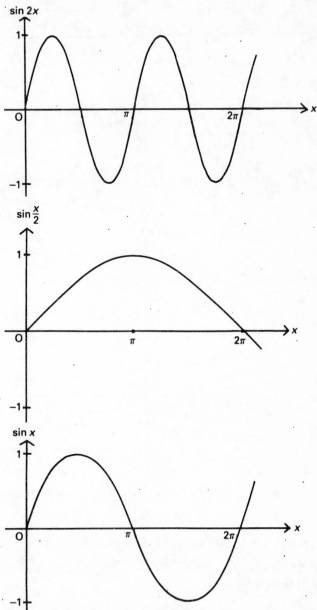

A worthwhile exercise would be to sketch the graphs of $\cos 2x$, $\cos x$ and $\cos \frac{x}{2}$ on the same scale.

GRAPHS OF SIN ($x \pm b$) and COS ($x \pm b$)

Note that the graph of sin x has been moved to the left by $\frac{\pi}{4}$.

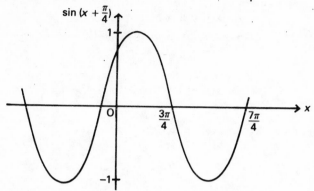

Note that the graph of cos x has been moved to the left by $\frac{\pi}{4}$.

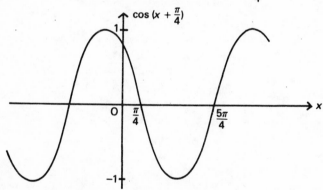

Note that the periods and amplitudes of the above are the same as for sin x and cos x.

The graph of sin ($x - b$) would be that of sin x moved b radians to the right.

The graph of cos ($x - b$) would be that of cos x moved b radians to the right.

The graph of sin ($ax + b$) would be the graph of sin x moved b radians to the left and with period $\frac{2\pi}{a}$.

The graph of cos ($ax - b$) would be the graph of cos x moved b radians to the right and with period $\frac{2\pi}{a}$.

Trigonometry

TRIGONOMETRY FORMULAE

The following formulae should be learned.

Sin $(A \pm B)$	$= \sin A \cos B \pm \cos A \sin B$
Cos $(A \pm B)$	$= \cos A \cos B \mp \sin A \sin B$
Sin 2A	$= 2 \sin A \cos A$
Cos 2A	$= \cos^2 A - \sin^2 A$
	$= 2 \cos^2 A - 1$ (since $\sin^2 A = 1 - \cos^2 A$)
	$= 1 - 2 \sin^2 A$ (since $\cos^2 A = 1 - \sin^2 A$)

Note that sin 2A
$$= \sin (A + A)$$
$$= \sin A \cos A + \cos A \sin A$$
$$= 2 \sin A \cos A$$

and cos 2A
$$= \cos (A + A)$$
$$= \cos A \cos A - \sin A \sin A$$
$$= \cos^2 A - \sin^2 A$$

Similarly sin 3A
$$= \sin (A + 2A)$$
$$= \sin A \cos 2A + \cos A \sin 2A$$
$$= \sin A(\cos^2 A - \sin^2 A) + \cos A(2 \sin A \cos A)$$
$$= \sin A \cos^2 A - \sin^3 A + 2 \cos^2 A \sin A$$
$$= 3 \sin A \cos^2 A - \sin^3 A$$
$$= 3 \sin A (1 - \sin^2 A) - \sin^3 A$$
$$= 3 \sin A - 4 \sin^3 A$$

SOLVING TRIGONOMETRIC EQUATIONS

Example

Solve $\cos^2 x - 3\cos x = -2$, $x \in R$.

First make one side of the equation zero giving
$\cos^2 x - 3\cos x + 2 = 0$
$(\cos x - 2)(\cos x - 1) = 0$
$\cos x = 2$ or $\cos x = 1$

Since the maximum value of a cosine is 1 there is only one solution
i.e. $\cos x = 1$

$\qquad x = 0$ or 2π or 4π etc., or -2π, -4π, etc.

In general $x \in \{2n\pi, n \in Z\}$

Example

Find solution set of $\sin 2x + \cos x = 0$, $0 \leqslant x \leqslant 2\pi$.

We first change the shape of the equation so as to express the left-hand side as a product of factors. Since 'cos x' is the simplest term we will try to change 'sin $2x$' into a form which has cos x as a factor.

$\qquad \sin 2x = 2\sin x \cos x$

Thus $\quad \sin 2x + \cos x = 0$

$\Leftrightarrow \quad 2\sin x \cos x + \cos x = 0$

$\Leftrightarrow \quad \cos x(2\sin x + 1) = 0$

$\Leftrightarrow \quad \cos x = 0$ or $2\sin x + 1 = 0$

$\qquad\qquad\qquad \Leftrightarrow \sin x = -\tfrac{1}{2}$

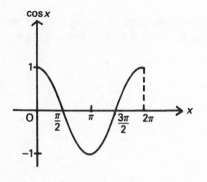 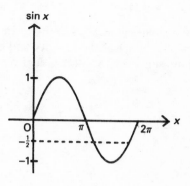

From the graphs we find the solution set to be $\left\{ \dfrac{\pi}{2}, \dfrac{3}{2}\pi, \dfrac{7}{6}\pi, \dfrac{11\pi}{6} \right\}$

Trigonometry

Note that in equations which give the situation where a common factor appears on both sides of the equation that factor cannot be cancelled else solutions will be lost, e.g.

$$\sin x \cos x = \cos x$$
$$\Leftrightarrow \quad \sin x \cos x - \cos x = 0$$
$$\Leftrightarrow \quad \cos x (\sin x - 1) = 0$$
$$\Leftrightarrow \quad \cos x = 0 \text{ or } \sin x = 1$$

The solution(s) for $\cos x = 0$ would have been lost if $\cos x$ had been cancelled in the first line.

Example

Prove that $\dfrac{\sin 2A}{1 + \cos 2A} = \tan A$

Note this form is called an identity and is true for all values of A.

$$\begin{aligned}
\text{L.H.S.} &= \frac{\sin A}{1 + \cos 2A} \\
&= \frac{2 \sin A \cos A}{1 + (2 \cos^2 A - 1)} \\
&= \frac{2 \sin A \cos A}{2 \cos^2 A} \\
&= \frac{\sin A}{\cos A} \\
&= \tan A \\
&= \text{R.H.S.}
\end{aligned}$$

Note that when asked to prove an identity we must start by taking the left hand side (L.H.S.) of the identity and change its form till it is the same as the right hand side (R.H.S.) of the identity.

$a \cos \theta + b \sin \theta$

It is often convenient to express $a \cos \theta + b \sin \theta$ in the form $r \cos (\theta - \alpha)$ where r is a positive constant and $0 \leqslant \alpha < 2\pi$.

First assume $a \cos \theta + b \sin \theta = r \cos (\theta - \alpha)$
$$= r \cos \theta \cos \alpha + r \sin \theta \sin \alpha$$
$$= (r \cos \alpha) \cos \theta + (r \sin \alpha) \sin \theta$$

Now by equating the coefficients of $\cos \theta$ and $\sin \theta$ on each side

$r \cos \alpha = a \Rightarrow r^2 \cos^2 \alpha = a^2$
$r \sin \alpha = b \Rightarrow r^2 \sin^2 \alpha = b^2$

By addition $r^2 \cos^2 \alpha + r^2 \sin^2 \alpha = a^2 + b^2$
$$r^2 (\cos^2 \alpha + \sin^2 \alpha) = a^2 + b^2$$
$$r^2 = a^2 + b^2$$
$$r = \sqrt{a^2 + b^2}$$

Also $\dfrac{r \sin \alpha}{r \cos \alpha} = \dfrac{b}{a}$

$\Leftrightarrow \qquad \tan \alpha = \dfrac{b}{a}$

The quadrant in which the auxiliary angle, α, lies is the same as that in which the point (a, b) lies.

The maximum and minimum values of $a \cos \theta + b \sin \theta$ are the maximum and minimum values of $r \cos(\theta - \alpha)$ and since the maximum value of $\cos(\theta - \alpha)$ is 1 then the maximum value is r. Similarly since the minimum value of $\cos(\theta - \alpha)$ is -1 then the minimum value is $-r$.

The value of θ for which the maximum and minimum values occur are found by solving the equations $\cos(\theta - \alpha) = 1$ and $\cos(\theta - \alpha) = -1$.

Trigonometry

THE EQUATION $a \cos \theta + b \sin \theta = c$

The equation $a \cos \theta + b \sin \theta = c$ is solved by first converting the L.H.S. to the form $r \cos(\theta - \alpha)$ giving:

$r \cos(\theta - \alpha) = c$

Thus $\cos(\theta - \alpha) = \dfrac{c}{r}$ which can be solved in the usual way.

Example

Solve the equation $3 \cos \theta° + 4 \sin \theta° = 5$ for $0 \leqslant \theta < 360$.

Let $3 \cos \theta° + 4 \sin \theta° = r \cos(\theta - \alpha)°$
$$= r \cos \theta° \cos \alpha° + r \sin \theta° \sin \alpha°$$

Thus $r \cos \alpha° = 3$ $\tan \alpha° = \frac{4}{3} = 1 \cdot 33$ (to 3 s.f.)

$\ r \sin \alpha° = 4$ $\alpha° = 53 \cdot 1°$ (to 3 s.f.)

$\ r = \sqrt{3^2 + 4^2} = 5$

Thus $5 \cos(\theta - 53 \cdot 1)° = 5$
$\Leftrightarrow \quad \cos(\theta - 53 \cdot 1)° = 1$
$\Leftrightarrow \quad (\theta - 53 \cdot 1) \quad\ = 0$
$\Leftrightarrow \quad \theta = 53 \cdot 1$ (to 3 s.f.)

DIFFERENTIATION

The gradient of $y = mx + c$ and $y = mx$ is m, and $m = \dfrac{y_2 - y_1}{x_2 - x_1} = \tan \theta$ where θ is the angle the line makes with the positive direction of the x-axis.

For the straight line, m is a constant and the value of c does not affect the gradient. The gradient tells us the rate of change of y with respect to x, e.g. if $m = \frac{3}{4}$ then for every 3 units that y changes then x will change by 4 units. This rate of change is the derivative of the function and is written $\dfrac{dy}{dx}$ when the function is $y = mx + c$ or $f'(x)$ when the function is referred to as $f(x) = mx + c$.

The gradient of a line can be referred to in many forms, e.g. m, $\dfrac{y_2 - y_1}{x_2 - x_1}$, $\tan \theta$, $\dfrac{dy}{dx}$, $f'(x)$ or, in words, the rate of change of y with respect to x, the derivative of y with respect to x or the derivative of the function. If $y = c$ or $f(x) = c$ then the line is parallel to the x-axis and its gradient is zero so $\dfrac{dy}{dx}$ or $f'(x) = 0$.

Now consider the case where the function is not represented by a straight line, as in the figure below where the rate of change of y with respect to x is not constant.

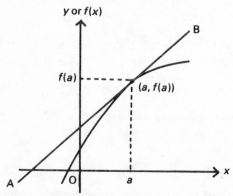

If we wish to know the rate of change at any point on this curve we will need a straight line at that point, i.e. a tangent at that point so that the gradient of the tangent will be the gradient of the curve at that point. The gradient found by the

Calculus

usual method $\dfrac{y_2 - y_1}{x_2 - x_1}$ or $\dfrac{f(x) - f(a)}{x - a}$ needs two points for the calculation yet our tangent meets the curve at only one point.

Our solution is to choose a point very close to $(a, f(a))$, i.e. $(a + h, f(a + h))$ where h is a value approaching zero. The gradient now becomes

$$\frac{f(a + h) - f(a)}{(a + h) - a} = \frac{f(a + h) - f(a)}{h}$$

i.e. the average rate of change of the function.

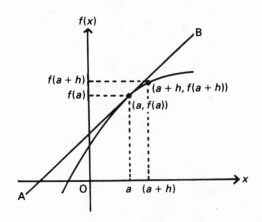

Now by taking the limit of this ratio as $h \to 0$ (h tends to zero) we have the required gradient of the function at the point $(a, f(a))$, i.e.

$$\frac{dy}{dx} \text{ or } f'(a) = \underset{h \to 0}{\text{Lim}} \frac{f(a + h) - f(a)}{h} \text{ or in general}$$

$$\frac{dy}{dx} \text{ or } f'(x) = \underset{h \to 0}{\text{Lim}} \frac{f(x + h) - f(x)}{h} \quad \begin{array}{l} \text{i.e. the instantaneous rate of change} \\ \text{of the function.} \end{array}$$

$\dfrac{dy}{dx}$ or $f'(x)$ is called the derived function or the derivative of y or $f(x)$.

The example on page 63 illustrates the above method of finding the derivative from first principles.

Example

Find the derivative of $f(x) = 2x + 3$ from first principles.

$f(x) = 2x + 3 \qquad f(x + h) = 2(x + h) + 3$

$f'(x) = \underset{h \to 0}{\text{Lim}} \dfrac{f(x + h) - f(x)}{h}$

$\quad = \underset{h \to 0}{\text{Lim}} \dfrac{[2(x + h) + 3] - [2x + 3]}{h}$

$\quad = \underset{h \to 0}{\text{Lim}} \dfrac{2x + 2h + 3 - 2x - 3}{h}$

$\quad = \underset{h \to 0}{\text{Lim}} \dfrac{2h}{h}$

$\quad = 2$

Notice again that 2 is the gradient of the line $f(x) = 2x + 3$, i.e. $m = f'(x)$

By considering the expansion of $(x + h)^n$ we arrive at a quick method of finding $f'(x)$ when $f(x) = x^n$.

$(x + h)^2 = x^2 + 2xh + h^2 \qquad\qquad = x^2 + 2xh + h^2$
$(x + h)^3 = x^3 + 3x^2h + 3xh^2 + h^3 \qquad = x^3 + 3x^2h + h^2(3x + h)$
$(x + h)^4 = x^4 + 4x^3h + 6x^2h^2 + 4xh^3 + h^4 = x^4 + 4x^3h + h^2(6x + 4xh + h^2)$
$(x + h)^n = x^n + nx^{n-1}h + h^2 \quad$ (Some expression in x)

From the above if $f(x) = x^n$, $n \in Q$ then

$f'(x) = \underset{h \to 0}{\text{Lim}} \dfrac{f(x + h) - f(x)}{h}$

$\quad = \underset{h \to 0}{\text{Lim}} \dfrac{x^n + nx^{n-1}h + h^2(\ldots\ldots)x^n}{h}$

$\quad = \underset{h \to 0}{\text{Lim}} \dfrac{nx^{n-1}h + h^2(\ldots\ldots)}{h}$

$\quad = \underset{h \to 0}{\text{Lim}}\, nx^{n-1} + h(\ldots\ldots)$

$\quad = nx^{n-1}$

The rule then is to multiply by the index and reduce the index by 1, e.g. $f(x) = x^4$ gives $f'(x) = 4x^3$. Similarly $f(x) = ax^5$, a is a constant, gives $f'(x) = 5ax^4$.

If $f(x)$ has several terms then each term is treated individually by the rule.

Calculus

Example

Find the derivative of $y = 3ax^4 - 2bx^3 + 5x - 7$.

$$\frac{dy}{dx} = 12ax^3 - 6bx^2 + 5$$

The following two derivatives should be memorised

$f(x) \;\;= \sin x$ $\qquad\qquad$ $f(x) \;\;= \cos x$

$f'(x) = \cos x$ $\qquad\qquad$ $f'(x) = -\sin x$

Compare this with the graphs given on page 50 and note that reading from the graph of $\cos x$ for any value of x will give the gradient of the tangent to the graph of $\sin x$ at that value of x.

INCREASING AND DECREASING INTERVALS, STATIONARY VALUES

When a tangent at a point on the graph of a function makes an acute angle with the positive direction of the x-axis we say the function is increasing at that point.

When the angle is obtuse we say the function is decreasing at that point.

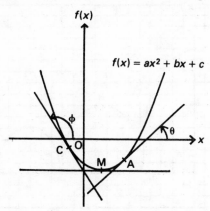

In short, a function is increasing at any point where the gradient of the tangent at that point is positive, because the tangent of an acute angle is positive. A function is decreasing at any point where the gradient of the tangent at that point is negative, because the tangent of an obtuse angle is negative.

Since $f'(x)$ is the gradient of a tangent we can write the above statements in symbols.

$f'(x) > 0 \Leftrightarrow f(x)$ is increasing

$f'(x) < 0 \Leftrightarrow f(x)$ is decreasing.

We are left now with the case where $f'(x) = 0$, i.e. at the point M in the above diagram. Notice that the tangent at M, the minimum value of $f(x)$ in this case, is parallel to the x-axis and so the angle between the tangent and the x-axis is $0°$.

At the minimum (or maximum) value of a function the tangent is parallel to the x-axis and so the gradient of the tangent at that point is zero, i.e. $f'(x) = 0$.

The value of a function at which $f'(x) = 0$ is said to be its turning value or its stationary value and the point at which this occurs is its turning point.

Consider the movement of a stone thrown into the air. Its height above the

Calculus

ground increases to a maximum then the stone becomes stationary before its height decreases as it falls to the ground.

It should be noted that a function can have a stationary value which is not the maximum or minimum value of the function, e.g. consider the path of a bouncing ball as illustrated in the following diagram.

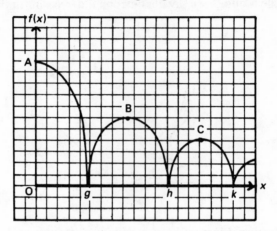

Here the maximum height of the ball is at A. B and C show the maximum heights reached after the first and second bounce. The tangents at these points are parallel to the x-axis so there are stationary values at B and C.

There is a maximum turning point at B but not the maximum value of the function. However at B is found the maximum in the closed interval $[g, h]$, i.e. where $g \leq x \leq h$. Similarly at C is found the maximum value in the closed interval $[h, k]$.

Maxima and minima are not the only types of stationary values in a function. Consider a rocket fired into the air whose second stage is fired just as the first stage reaches its maximum height. This might be depicted as the following graph.

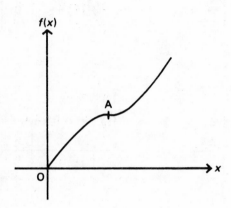

At the point A the rocket ceases to rise from the first stage boost but just as the thrust ends the second stage fires and causes the rocket to rise further. Such a stationary point is called a point of inflexion.

Notice that at a point of inflexion the graph does not change from an increasing to a decreasing part of the function but that it increases up to the stationary value at the point of inflexion and then continues to increase from there.

A point of inflexion can occur when a function decreases then tapers off to a stationary value then decreases again.

All points of inflexion need not be stationary values but only those whose tangent at that point is parallel to the x-axis, i.e. when $f'(x) = 0$.

Calculus

The following tables are useful in determining the nature of a turning point.

Minimum

If $f'(x) = 0$ when $x = a$

	a^-	a	a^+
$f'(x) -$		0	+
	$\searrow$	$\rightarrow$	$\nearrow$

Maximum

If $f'(x) = 0$ when $x = a$

	a^-	a	a^+
$f'(x) +$		0	−
	$\nearrow$	$\rightarrow$	$\searrow$

Points of inflexion

Decreasing

If $f'(x) = 0$ when $x = a$

	a^-	a	a^+
$f'(x) -$		0	−
	$\searrow$	$\rightarrow$	$\searrow$

Increasing

If $f'(x) = 0$ when $x = a$

	a^-	a	a^+
$f'(x) +$		0	+
	$\nearrow$	$\rightarrow$	$\nearrow$

Example

Find the stationary values of the function f defined by $f(x) = x^2(x-1)^2$ and determine their nature. Sketch the graph of the function.

$$f(x) = x^2(x-1)^2$$
$$= x^2(x^2 - 2x + 1)$$
$$= x^4 - 2x^3 + x^2$$

$$f'(x) = 4x^3 - 6x^2 + 2x$$
$$= 2x(2x^2 - 3x + 1)$$
$$= 2x(2x - 1)(x - 1)$$

$f'(x) = 0$ when $x = 0$ or $x = \frac{1}{2}$ or $x = 1$

x	0^-	0	0^+
$2x$	$-$	0	$+$
$(2x-1)$	$-$	$-$	$-$
$(x-1)$	$-$	$-$	$-$
$f'(x)$	$\searrow$	0	$\nearrow$

Minimum Stationary
$(0, 0)$

x	$\frac{1}{2}^-$	$\frac{1}{2}$	$\frac{1}{2}^+$
$2x$	$+$	$+$	$+$
$(2x-1)$	$-$	0	$+$
$(x-1)$	$-$	$-$	$-$
$f'(x)$	$+$ $\nearrow$	0 $\rightarrow$	$-$ $\searrow$

Maximum Stationary
$(\frac{1}{2}, \frac{1}{16})$

x	1^-	1	1^+
$2x$	$+$	$+$	$+$
$(2x-1)$	$+$	$+$	$+$
$(x-1)$	$-$	0	$+$
$f'(x)$	$\searrow$	0	$\nearrow$

Minimum Stationary
$(1, 0)$

When $x = 0$, $f(0) = 0$ so graph goes through the origin.

When $f(x) = 0$, $x^2(x-1)^2 = 0 \Leftrightarrow x = 0$ or $x = 1$.

When x is a large positive value $f(x)$ is large and positive.

When x is a large negative value $f(x)$ is large and positive.

Calculus

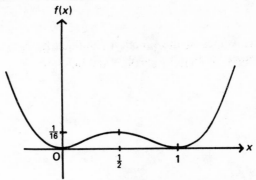

Note that when $f(x)$ has a factor which is a square then the x-axis will be a tangent to the curve at the value of x which makes that factor zero as for $x = 0$ and $x = 1$ above from the factors x^2 and $(x - 1)^2$ respectively.

Example

Determine the interval for which the function $f(x) = \frac{1}{3}x^3 - x^2 - 3x + 3$ is

(a) increasing,   *(b)* decreasing

$f'(x) = x^2 - 2x - 3$

$\qquad = (x + 1)(x - 3)$

Here it is advisable to sketch the curve of $f'(x)$ which is NOT the same as the curve $f(x)$.

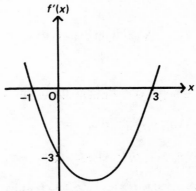

The function $f(x)$ is increasing when $f'(x) > 0$, i.e. $-1 > x$ or $x > 3$.

The function $f(x)$ is decreasing when $f'(x) < 0$, i.e. $-1 < x < 3$.

When dealing with a closed interval of a function then the maximum or minimum value need not be a stationary value of the function, e.g. in the diagram below the maximum value of the function is at $f(a)$, and the minimum at $f(b)$, if we deal with the closed interval $[a, b]$.

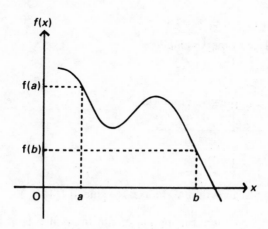

It should be realised that not all functions are differentiable. A function, f, is differentiable when the domain of f is the domain of f'.

Calculus

Example

Find the maximum and minimum values of $f : x \to 2x - x^2$ in $\left[-1, \frac{3}{2} \right]$.
Sketch the graph.

$$f(x) = 2x - x^2$$
$$f'(x) = 2 - 2x$$
$$= 2(1 - x) = 0 \Leftrightarrow x = 1.$$

Thus the only stationary value is:

$$f(1) = 2(1) - (1)^2$$
$$= 1.$$

This value lies in the given interval.

x	1^-	1	1^+
$1 - x$	$+$	0	$-$
$f'(x) = 2(1 - x)$	$+$	0	$-$
	$\nearrow$	$\to$	$\searrow$

Thus $x = 1$ gives a maximum stationary value of $f(1) = 1$.

The values of f at the end points of the interval $[-1, \frac{3}{2}]$ are $f(-1) = -3$ and $f(\frac{3}{2}) = \frac{3}{4}$.

Thus the minimum value in the interval is -3.

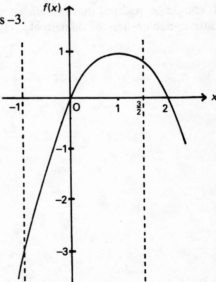

Thus $-3 \leqslant f(x) \leqslant 1$.

Notice that the maximum and minimum values asked for are those of the function, i.e. $f(x)$ not the values of x.

Example

Find the equation of the tangent to the curve $f(x) = x^2 + 3$ at the point where $x = 2$.

(i) The point on the line is $(2, f(2))$. By substitution in the given function $f(2) = 2^2 + 3 = 7$ so the point is $(2, 7)$.

(ii) The gradient $m = f'(x) = 2x \Rightarrow f'(2) = 2.2 = 4$.

(iii) The required equation by substitution in the form
$y - b = m(x - a)$ is $y - 7 = 4(x - 2) \Leftrightarrow y = 4x - 1$.

Example

Find the equation of the tangent(s) to the curve $f(x) = x^3 - 3x^2 - 3x + 2$ whose gradient is 6.

$f(x) = x^3 - 3x^2 - 3x + 2$
$f'(x) = 3x^2 - 6x - 3$

Since $f'(x) = m = 6$ then

$3x^2 - 6x - 3 = 6$
$\Leftrightarrow 3x^2 - 6x - 9 = 0$
$\Leftrightarrow 3(x^2 - 2x - 3) = 0$
$\Leftrightarrow 3(x + 1)(x - 3) = 0$
$\Leftrightarrow x = -1 \text{ or } x = 3$
$\Leftrightarrow$ The tangents of gradient 6 occur at $x = -1$ and $x = 3$.

Now when $x = -1$ $f(-1) = 1$
and when $x = 3$ $f(3) = -7$
i.e. $m = 6$ at points $(-1, 1)$ and $(3, -7)$.

The equation of the tangents at these points are:
$y - 1 = 6(x + 1)$ and $y + 7 = 6(x - 3)$
$\Leftrightarrow y = 6x + 7$ and $y = 6x - 25$.

Calculus

INTEGRATION

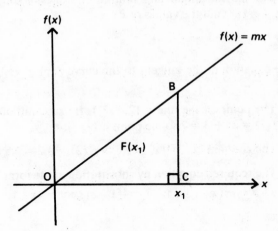

Area of triangle OBC $= F(x_1)$
$$= \tfrac{1}{2}x_1 m x_1$$
$$= \tfrac{1}{2}m x_1^2$$
But $F'(x_1) = m x_1$
$$= f(x_1)$$

$m x_1$ is the derivative of $\tfrac{1}{2}m x_1^2$ with respect to x.

$\tfrac{1}{2}m x_1^2$ is the integral of $m x_1$ with respect to x.

The integral of $f(x)$ with respect to x is written $\int f(x)\,dx$.

The integral of a function gives the area between the line (or curve) and the x-axis.

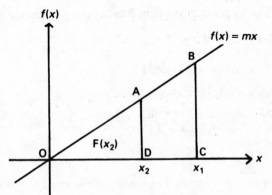

Area ABCD = Area OBC − Area OAD = $F(x_1) - F(x_2)$
$$= \tfrac{1}{2}mx_1^2 - \tfrac{1}{2}mx_2^2$$
But $F'(x_1) - F'(x_2) = mx_1 - mx_2$
$$= f(x_1) - f(x_2)$$

The area between the curve and the x-axis between x_1 and x_2 is the integral of $f(x)$ with respect to x from the lower limit x_2 to the upper limit x_1, i.e.

$$\int_{x_2}^{x_1} f(x)\,dx = F(x_1) - F(x_2)$$

Integration may be considered as the inverse operation of differentiation. For example to differentiate the form x^n the following steps were taken:

1. Subtract the constant.
2. Multiply x^n by the index.
3. Subtract 1 from the index.

The inverse of this for integration of x^n.

1. Add 1 to the index.
2. Divide x^{n+1} by the index.
3. Add a constant.

Thus

$$\int x^n dx = \frac{x^{n+1}}{n+1} + C.$$

An exception to this rule is when $n = -1$ for then

$$\int x^{-1} dx = \frac{x^{-1+1}}{-1+1} + C = \frac{1}{0} + C \text{ but the form } \frac{1}{0} \text{ is undefined.}$$

When limits of integration are involved we are dealing with a definite integral, e.g. $\int_1^2 x^n dx$. Here the '1' is the lower limit and the '2' the upper limit of integration.

$$\int_1^2 x^n dx = \left[\frac{x^{n+1}}{n+1}\right]_1^2$$
$$= \left[\frac{2^{n+1}}{n+1}\right] - \left[\frac{1^{n+1}}{n+1}\right]$$
$$= \frac{2^{n+1} - 1}{n+1}$$

Note that no constant of integration is required when dealing with a definite integral.

Calculus

Notes

1. $\int f(x)\, dx$ is called the indefinite integral, i.e. when no limits are given. In such a case a constant of integration must be added, e.g. $\int x^2\, dx = \frac{x^3}{3} + C$. The value of 'C' is not known without further information.

2. $\int kf(x)\, dx = k \int f(x)\, dx$, where k is any constant.

3. $\int [f(x) + g(x)]\, dx = \int f(x)\, dx + \int g(x)\, dx$.

4. $\int_a^b f(x)\, dx + \int_b^c f(x)\, dx = \int_a^c f(x)\, dx$.

5. $\int_a^b f(x)\, dx = -\int_b^a f(x)\, dx$.

Before attempting to integrate any function it is advisable to ensure that it is in the form of a sum or difference of terms each of the shape ax^n.

$$\int \frac{(x^2 + x)^2}{x}\, dx = \int \frac{x^4 + 2x^3 + x^2}{x}\, dx$$
$$= \int \left(\frac{x^4}{x} + \frac{2x^3}{x} + \frac{x^2}{x} \right) dx$$
$$= \int (x^3 + 2x^2 + x)\, dx$$
$$= \frac{x^4}{4} + \frac{2x^3}{3} + \frac{x^2}{2} + C.$$

Cautions

1. When integrating a single function to find the area between the curve and the x-axis, first check whether for any values between the given limits the curve crosses the x-axis.

   e.g.

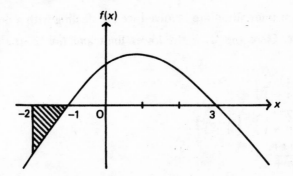

In the diagram the shaded area is below the x-axis and so the value of $f(x)$

will be negative. If then it is necessary to find the area between the curve and the x-axis from $x = -2$ to $x = 3$, i.e. $\int_{-2}^{3} f(x)\,dx$ we should split the integral into two parts viz. $\int_{-2}^{-1} f(x)\,dx$ and $\int_{-1}^{3} f(x)\,dx$ and on evaluation sum the magnitudes of the integrals.

2. If the area between two curves is involved there is no need to worry about the crossing of the x-axis as long as $f(x) \geqslant g(x)$ for $a \leqslant x \leqslant b$, e.g. to find the area between $f(x)$ and $g(x)$:

   (a) If possible make a sketch.

   (b) Find the points of intersection.

   (c) Use these points as limits, say a and b.

   (d) Evaluate $\int_{a}^{b} [f(x) - g(x)]\,dx$, where $g(x)$ would be the lower curve of the sketch over the enclosed area.

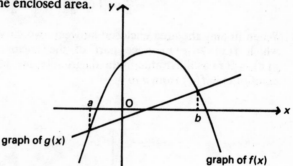

3. Note the difference between being asked to

   (a) evaluate $\int_{0}^{2} (x^3 - 3x^2 + 2x)\,dx$ and

   (b) find the area between the curve $x^3 - 3x^2 + 2x$ and the x-axis from $x = 0$ to $x = 2$.

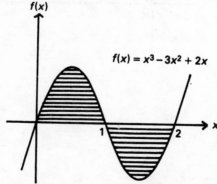

Calculus

The answer to (a) is 0, but obviously, from the sketch the area asked for is the shaded region, which is not 0.

(a) $\int_0^2 (x^3 - 3x^2 + 2x)\, dx = \left[\frac{x^4}{4} - x^3 + x^2 \right]_0^2$

$= \frac{16}{4} - 8 + 4 - 0$

$= 0$

(b) $\int_0^2 (x^3 - 3^2 + 2x)\, dx = \int_0^1 (x^3 - 3x^2 + 2x)\, dx + \left| \int_1^2 (x^3 - 3x^2 + 2x)\, dx \right|$

$= \left[\frac{x^4}{4} - x^3 + x^2 \right]_0^1 + \left| \left[\frac{x^4}{4} - x^3 + x^2 \right]_1^2 \right|$

$= \left[\frac{1}{4} - 1 + 1 \right] - 0 + \left| \left[\frac{16}{4} - 8 + 4 \right] - \left[\frac{1}{4} - 1 + 1 \right] \right|$

$= \frac{1}{4} + \left| \left[0 - \frac{1}{4} \right] \right| = \frac{1}{4} + \frac{1}{4} = \frac{1}{2} \text{ units}^2.$

4. When finding the area enclosed between two curves check the limits within which $f(x) \geqslant g(x)$ since part of the enclosed area could be where $g(x) \geqslant f(x)$ as illustrated in the diagram below. Here $f(x) \geqslant g(x)$ from 0 to a but $g(x) \geqslant f(x)$ from a to b.

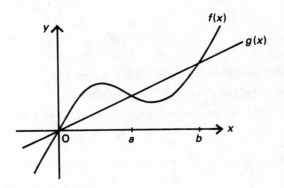

Example

Find the area of the region in the first quadrant which is bounded by the line $y = x$ and the curve $y = x^3$

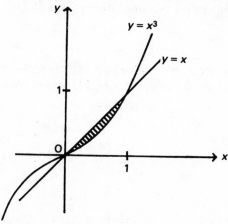

The required area is shaded in the above diagram. The curves intersect in the first quadrant when $x = 0$ and when $x = 1$.

$$A = \int_0^1 (x - x^3)\, dx$$
$$= [\tfrac{1}{2}x^2 - \tfrac{1}{4}x^4]_0^1 = \tfrac{1}{2} - \tfrac{1}{4} = \tfrac{1}{4}\ \text{units}^2$$

If we were now asked to find the total area between the two curves in the above example then because of the symmetry of the figure we would know that the area in the third quadrant would be equal to that in the first quadrant so the total area is $2 \int_0^1 (x - x^3)\, dx = \tfrac{1}{2}\ \text{units}^2$.

Note that $\int_{-1}^1 (x - x^3)\, dx = 0$ and $\int_{-1}^0 (x - x^3)\, dx = -\tfrac{1}{4}$

Example

If the rate of change of y with respect to x is $3x^2 + 4x + 3$ and $y = 1$ when $x = 0$ find y.

$\dfrac{dy}{dx} = 3x^2 + 4x + 3$

$y\ = x^3 + 2x^2 + 3x + c$

$1\ = 0 + 0 + 0 + c$

$c\ = 1$

$y\ = x^3 + 2x^2 + 3x + 1$

Calculus

Example

The rate of separation, s, of two spacecraft is known to be proportional to the difference in their distances, d_1 and d_2, from earth. Write down an equation to use in finding their separation after a given time.

$$\frac{ds}{dt} = k(d_2 - d_1)$$

Here we would substitute for d_1 and d_2 in terms of t then integrate with respect to t. The value of k would be found if we substitute a known value of s for some given t.

LIST OF DERIVATIVES AND INTEGRALS

$f(x)$	$f'(x)$	$\int f(x)\,dx$
x^n	nx^{n-1}	$\dfrac{x^{n+1}}{n+1}, n \neq -1$
ax^n	nax^{n-1}	$\dfrac{ax^{n+1}}{n+1}, n \neq -1$
$\sin x$	$\cos x$	$-\cos x$
$\cos x$	$-\sin x$	$\sin x$
$\sin ax$	$a\cos ax$	$-\dfrac{1}{a}\cos ax$
$\cos ax$	$-a\sin ax$	$\dfrac{1}{a}\sin ax$
$\sin(ax+b)$	$a\cos(ax+b)$	$-\dfrac{1}{a}\cos(ax+b)$
$\cos(ax+b)$	$-a\sin(ax+b)$	$\dfrac{1}{a}\sin(ax+b)$
$(ax+b)^n$	$na(ax+b)^{n-1}$	$\dfrac{(ax+b)^{n+1}}{a(n+1)}, n \neq -1$

Note that if $f(x) = g(h(x))$ then $f'(x) = g'(h(x)).h'(x)$

WHAT'S THE DIFFERENCE? AN INVESTIGATION

A pupil told the teacher that the values of $f(x)$ for a certain quadratic expression were $f(x) = 5, 9, 15, 23, 33, 44$ for $x = 0, 1, 2, 3, 4, 5$ respectively. The teacher then wrote the following on the board and told the pupil there was an error. Investigate.

x	$f(x)$		
0	5		
		4	
1	9		2
		6	
2	15		2
		8	
3	23		2
		10	
4	33		1
		11	
5	44		

Since $f(x)$ is a quadratic then $f(x) = ax^2 + bx + c$, but no values for a, b nor c have been given. However when $x = 0$, $f(x) = 5$ so the value of the constant c is easily found and now $f(x) = ax^2 + bx + 5$.

From the pattern on the board we suspect that the final entry in the last column should also be a 2 and this is how the teacher knew there was an error.

Examination of the columns shows that the last two come by taking the difference between the entries in the previous column. This observation can be used to 'correct' the entries.

x	$f(x)$	1st diff	2nd diff.
0	5		
		4	
1	9		2
		6	
2	15		2
		8	
3	23		2
		10	
4	33		2
		12	
5	45		

By substitution in $f(x) = ax^2 + bx + 5$

then $\qquad f(1) = a + b + 5 = 9$

and $\qquad f(2) = 4a + 2b + 5 = 15$

giving $\qquad \left.\begin{array}{l} a + b = 4 \\ 2a + b = 5 \end{array}\right\} \Rightarrow \begin{array}{l} a = 1 \\ b = 3 \end{array}$

so $\qquad f(x) = x^2 + 3x + 5$

So far the procedure has been to examine the data, find a pattern, form a conjecture and test the conjecture. The original quadratic has been found but nothing is known yet as to how the pattern and the values of a, b and c are connected. More quadratics will have to be examined with different values for a, b and c and then an attempt to generalise will be made.

Examples with different values for a, b and c:

1. $f(x) = 2x^2 + 3x + 5$

x	$f(x)$	1st diff.	2nd diff.
0	5		
		5	
1	10		4
		9	
2	19		4
		13	
3	32		4
		17	
4	49		

2. $f(x) = 3x^2 + 3x + 5$

x	$f(x)$	1st diff.	2nd diff
0	5		
		6	
1	11		6
		12	
2	23		6
		18	
3	41		

It seems that the second difference is always twice the coefficient of x^2 and the value of the constant is always the first entry in the $f(x)$ column.

What's the Difference? An Investigation

To test this conjecture we use $f(x) = 4x^2 + 3x + 1$ and predict that the last column will be 8's and the first value of $f(x)$ will be 1.

x	$f(x)$	1st diff.	2nd diff.
0	1		
		7	
1	8		8
		15	
2	23		8
		23	
3	46		

We now try to be more general and use $f(x) = ax^2 + bx + c$

x	$f(x)$	1st diff	2nd diff
0	$\boxed{c}$		
		$a + \boxed{b}$	
1	$a + b + c$		$2\boxed{a}$
		$3a + b$	
2	$4a + 2b + c$		$2a$
		$5a + b$	
3	$9a + 3b + c$		

It is now clear that the value of b, the coefficient of x can be found by subtracting a from the first entry in the 1st difference column.

The investigation can be carried further by examining
$f(x) = ax^3 + bx^2 + cx + d$

x	$f(x)$	1st diff.	2nd diff.	3rd diff.
0	d			
		$a + b + c$		
1	$a + b + c + d$		$6a + 2b$	
		$7a + 3b + c$		$6a$
2	$8a + 4b + 2c + d$		$12a + 2b$	
		$19a + 5b + c$		$6a$
3	$27a + 9b + 3c + d$		$18a + 2b$	
		$37a + 7b + c$		
4	$64a + 16b + 4c + d$			

Whereas quadratics required 2 differences to reach a multiple of a, the cubic needs 3 differences. From this it could be predicted and tested that $f(x) = ax^4 + bx^3 + cx^2 + dx + e$ would need 4 differences. From here the final difference columns could be listed

$$a = 1 \times a \qquad \text{when } f(x) = ax + b$$
$$2a = 1 \times 2 \times a \qquad \text{when } f(x) = ax^2 + bx + c$$
$$6a = 1 \times 2 \times 3 \times a \qquad \text{when } f(x) = ax^3 + bx^2 + cx + d$$
$$24a = 1 \times 2 \times 3 \times 4 \times a \qquad \text{when } f(x) = ax^4 + bx^3 + cx^2 + dx + e$$
$$n\,!\,a = 1 \times 2 \times 3 \ldots \ldots \times n \times a \quad \text{when } f(x) = ax^n + bx^{n-1} + \ldots\ldots\ldots\ldots\ldots$$

It is of interest to note that when

$$f(x) = ax + b \qquad f'(x) = a$$
$$f(x) = ax^2 + bx + c \qquad f''(x) = 2a$$
$$f(x) = ax^3 + bx^2 + cx + d \quad f'''(x) = 6a$$
$$f(x) = ax^n + bx^{n-1} + \ldots\ldots \quad f^n(x) = n!\,a$$

i.e. the nth differential of a polynomial is equal to the nth difference and is a constant.

The investigation has come a long way from finding the a, b and c for the original quadratic expression and could be taken a lot further, e.g. to find the coefficients b, c, etc. in polynomial expressions of degree greater than 2. How far any investigation is taken is the decision one must make for oneself.

The difference procedure used above can help solve such problems as the following:

> How many cables are needed so that 100 computers can be joined directly to each other when only one cable is needed to join any two computers together?

First draw some diagrams dealing with a small number of computers.

Now tabulate the results.

Number of computers	Number of cables
0	0
1	0
2	1
3	3
4	6
5	10

What's the Difference? An Investigation

The number of cables already exhibits a pattern, viz the sequence of triangular numbers but it would take a long time to reach the hundredth entry in this sequence. The difference method will be applied to the number of cables.

Number of computers	Number of cables	1st diff.	2nd diff.
0	0	0	1
1	0	1	1
2	1	2	1
3	3	3	1
4	6	4	
5	10		

Since only two differences are required we know that the function is a quadratic, i.e. $f(n) = an^2 + bn + c$ and that $a = \frac{1}{2}$ and $b = -\frac{1}{2}$ and $c = 0$ so

$$f(n) = \frac{1}{2}n^2 - \frac{1}{2}n$$
$$= \frac{1}{2}n(n-1)$$

We can now test this formula against the results table. Thus having found the general solution we can substitute $n = 100$ to find the solution to the original question, i.e. 4950 cables are required.

SPECIMEN QUESTIONS WITH SOLUTIONS

N.B. You are advised to attempt to solve these questions on your own and then compare your results with the given solutions.

1. Find the equation of the tangent to the curve $y = k\sqrt{x}$ at the point where $x = p$.

   Solution:

   The tangent to a curve is a straight line and so its equation can be found if the gradient and a point on the line are known. (See page 40 (2))

   The gradient, m, will be $\dfrac{dy}{dx}$ (see page 61).

   Since $y = kx^{\frac{1}{2}}$

   $$\frac{dy}{dx} = \frac{k}{2}x^{-\frac{1}{2}} = \frac{k}{2\sqrt{p}} \text{ at } x = p$$

   The point on the line is $(p, k\sqrt{p})$

   Using $y - b = m(x - a)$

   $$y - k\sqrt{p} = \frac{k}{2\sqrt{p}}(x - p)$$

   Note: values for k and p might be given in the question.

2. If $\sin A = \dfrac{\sqrt{3}}{2}$ $\left(0 < A < \dfrac{\pi}{2}\right)$ find exact values of cos A and sin 2A.

   Solution

   Angle A is given in radian measure (see page 49).

   Using the ratios of a right angled triangle the cos A can be read once the theorem of Pythagoras has been used to find the third side.

   $\cos A = \dfrac{1}{2}$

   $\sin 2A = 2 \sin A \cos A$
   (see page 56)

   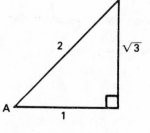

   $$= 2 \cdot \frac{\sqrt{3}}{2} \cdot \frac{1}{2} = \frac{\sqrt{3}}{2}$$

Specimen Questions with Solutions

Note: $\sin A = \sin 2A = \dfrac{\sqrt{3}}{2}$ because $A = \dfrac{\pi}{3}$ and so $2A = \dfrac{2\pi}{3}$ i.e. the supplement of A (see page 49).

Calculators must **not** be used when exact values are required.

3. Find the x co-ordinates of the points where the line with equation $y = mx + c$ cuts the circle with equation $x^2 + y^2 = r^2$

Solution:

$x^2 + y^2 = r^2$ is the equation of circle radius r and centre O, the origin (see page 42).

The equations may be solved simultaneously by substitution (see page 46).

$$x^2 + (mx + c)^2 = r^2$$
$$\Leftrightarrow \ x^2 + m^2x^2 + 2mcx + c^2 = r^2$$
$$\Leftrightarrow \ x^2(1 + m^2) + 2mcx + (c^2 - r^2) = 0$$

The above equation is of the form $ax^2 + bx + c = 0$

so $x = \dfrac{-2mc \pm \sqrt{(2mc)^2 - 4(1 + m^2)(c^2 - r^2)}}{2(1 + m^2)}$ (See pages 12 – 15.)

Note: values for m, c and r might be given in this type of question.

4. Find the values of θ $(0 \leqslant \theta \leqslant \pi)$ for which $v = a \sin\left(n\theta - \dfrac{\pi}{4}\right)$ has its maximum value. Do **not** use calculus.

Solution:

The maximum value of the sine of an angle is 1 (see page 50) so

$$\sin\left(n\theta - \dfrac{\pi}{4}\right) = 1$$

$$\Rightarrow \ n\theta - \dfrac{\pi}{4} = \dfrac{\pi}{2}, \dfrac{\pi}{2} + 2\pi, \dfrac{\pi}{2} + 4\pi \quad \text{(See page 50 on periodicity.)}$$

$$= \dfrac{\pi}{2} + 2k\pi, k \in z$$

$$= \pi\left(\dfrac{4k + 1}{2}\right)$$

$\Rightarrow \; n\theta \quad = \pi\left(\dfrac{4k+1}{2}\right) + \dfrac{\pi}{4} = \dfrac{\pi}{4}(8k+3)$

$\Rightarrow \; \theta \quad = \dfrac{\pi}{4n}(8k+3)$

$\Rightarrow \; 0 \leqslant \dfrac{8k+3}{4n} \leqslant 1$

Note: values for a and n might be given in this type of question.

5. $\dfrac{dy}{dx} = ax + b$ for all points on a curve.

   If the curve passes through the point (p, q) find the equation of the curve.

   Solution:

   Integration is the inverse operation of differentiation (see pages 75 and 79).

   Thus $y = \dfrac{ax^2}{2} + bx + c$

   Since (p, q) lies on the curve

   $\quad q = \dfrac{ap^2}{2} + bp + c$

   $\Leftrightarrow \; c = q - \dfrac{ap^2}{2} - bp$

   Note: values for a, b, p, q might be given in this type of question.

6. Find the stationary values of the function $f(x) = ax + \dfrac{b}{x}$ $(x \neq 0)$ and determine the nature of each.

   Solution:

   Stationary values occur when $f'(x) = 0$ (see pages 65 – 69).

   $\quad f'(x) = a - \dfrac{b}{x^2}$ (See page 63, last four lines.)

   $\quad\quad = 0$ when $a = \dfrac{b}{x^2}$

   $\quad\quad \Rightarrow \; x^2 = \dfrac{b}{a}$

   $\quad\quad\quad x = \pm \sqrt{\dfrac{b}{a}}$

Specimen Questions with Solutions

The nature of the stationary values can be found by the method shown on pages 68 and 69, e.g. if $b = 1$ and $a = 4$ then $x = \pm\frac{1}{2} \Leftrightarrow f'(x) = 0$

x	$\frac{1}{2}^-$	$\frac{1}{2}$	$\frac{1}{2}^+$		$-\frac{1}{2}^-$	$-\frac{1}{2}$	$-\frac{1}{2}^+$
$f'(x)$	$-$	0	$+$		$+$	0	$-$
	$\searrow$	$\rightarrow$	$\nearrow$		$\nearrow$	$\rightarrow$	$\searrow$
		minimum at $x = \frac{1}{2}$				maximum at $x = -\frac{1}{2}$	

The maximum stationary value of $f(x) = 4x + \dfrac{1}{x}$ is $4 \times \left(\dfrac{-1}{2}\right) + \dfrac{1}{-\frac{1}{2}} = -4$

The minimum stationary value is $4 \times \frac{1}{2} + \dfrac{1}{\frac{1}{2}} = 4$

Notice that a maximum stationary value need not be the maximum value of a function and similarly with a minimum stationary value (see page 66).

7. Evaluate $\displaystyle\int_{-2}^{3}(2x + 3)\,dx$ and draw a diagram to interpret this as an area of a region in the x, y-plane.

Solution:

$$\int_{-2}^{3}(2x + 3)\,dx = [x^2 + 3x]_{-2}^{3}$$
$$= [3^2 + 9] - [(-2)^2 + (-6)]$$
$$= 18 - [4 - 6]$$
$$= 20$$

The area required comprises $\triangle ABC - \triangle CDE$ (see pages 77 – 78)

i.e. $\frac{1}{2}(4\cdot5)(9) - \frac{1}{2}(0\cdot5)(1) = 20\cdot25 - 0\cdot25$
$$= 20 \text{ units}^2$$

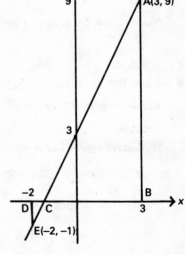

8. The following information about a curve has been obtained.

    (a) It passes through the origin.
    (b) It passes through the points $(\pm 1 \cdot 5, 0)$.
    (c) It has a maximum turning point at $(1, 2)$.
    (d) It has a minimum turning value of -5 where $x = -1$.

    Sketch a curve to satisfy these conditions.

    Solution:

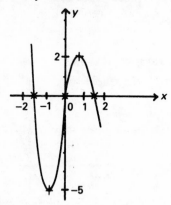

    The significant points given in (a) to (d) above are marked by crosses on the diagram (see pages 66 – 69).

9. Show that for triangle PQR $\quad p = \dfrac{q \sin \alpha}{\cos (\theta - \alpha)}$

    Solution:

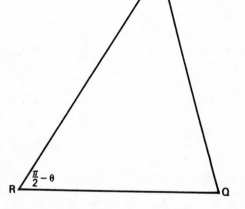

    Notice that $\dfrac{p}{\sin \alpha} = \dfrac{q}{\sin Q}$

    $\Leftrightarrow p = \dfrac{q \sin \alpha}{\sin Q}$

Specimen Questions with Solutions

If it can be shown that $\cos(\theta - \alpha) = \sin Q$ the problem is solved.

$$Q = \pi - \left(\frac{\pi}{2} - \theta + \alpha\right) \text{ by sum of angles of a triangle}$$

$$= \left(\frac{\pi}{2} + \theta - \alpha\right)$$

$$\sin Q = \sin\left[\frac{\pi}{2} + (\theta - \alpha)\right] \text{ (see page 50)}$$

$$= \cos(\theta - \alpha)$$

10 The graph of $y = f(x)$, $-4 \leqslant x \leqslant 4$ is shown.
Sketch on separate diagrams the graphs of

(a) $y = -f(x)$
(b) $y = a + f(x)$

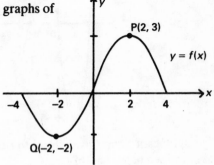

Solution:

(a) $y = -f(x)$ is a reflection of $y = f(x)$ is the x-axis.

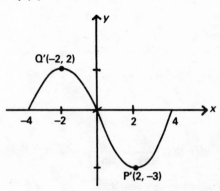

92

(b) $y = a + f(x)$ is a translation of the graph of $y = f(x)$ by a units parallel to the y-axis.

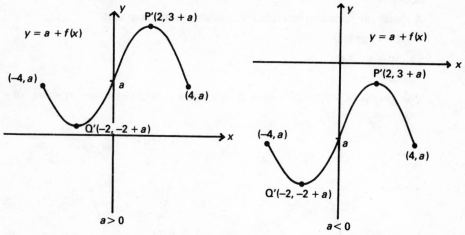

11. *(a)* Write down the first 5 terms of the sequence given by the recurrence relation $U_{r+1} = KU_r\ (r \geqslant 0)$ when $U_0 = 5$ and K is a constant.

(b) Give the general formula for U_n

Solution:

(a) $U_1 = KU_0 \Rightarrow U_1 = 5K$ (see page 6)

$U_2 = KU_1 \Rightarrow U_2 = 5K^2$

$U_3 = KU_2 \Rightarrow U_3 = 5K^3$

$U_4 = KU_3 \Rightarrow U_4 = 5K^4$

$U_5 = KU_4 \Rightarrow U_5 = 5K^5$

(b) $U_n = KU_{n-1} \Rightarrow U_n = 5K^n$

12. Show that the function $f(x) = 3x^3 - 3x^2 + x + 1$ is never decreasing.

Solution:

$f(x)$ is decreasing when $f'(x) < 0$ (see page 65).

$f'(x) = 9x^2 - 6x + 1$

$\quad\quad\ = (3x - 1)^2$

Since the square of any real number is positive or zero $f'(x) \geqslant 0$ thus $f(x)$ is never decreasing.

93

Specimen Questions with Solutions

13. For what values of p does the equation $x^2 - 4x + p = 0$ have real roots.

Solution:

A quadratic equation has real roots when the discriminant

$$b^2 - 4ac \geqslant 0$$

i.e. $16 - 4p \geqslant 0$

$$\Leftrightarrow \quad p \leqslant 4.$$

The graphs of $f(x) = x^2 - 4x + p$ illustrate the effect of different values of p (see pages 12 – 13).

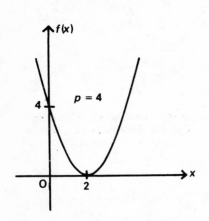

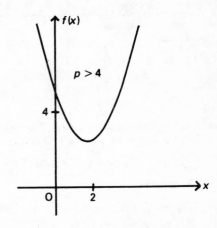

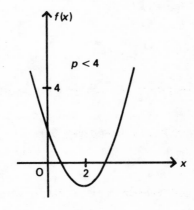

14. The sketch of the graph of a cubic function $y = f(x)$ is shown. Sketch the graph of $f'(x)$.

Solution:

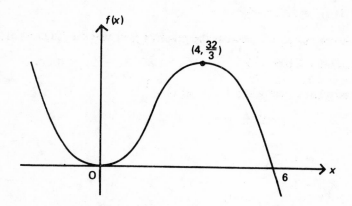

Since $f(x)$ is a cubic function then $f'(x)$ will be quadratic and its graph a parabola which will cut the x-axis at $x = 0$ and $x = 4$ since these are the values of x at which $f(x)$ has turning points, i.e. a minimum at $x = 0$ and maximum at $x = 4$.

Since $f(x)$ is increasing for $0 < x < 4$ then $f'(x)$ will be positive in this range. (See pages 65 – 69.)

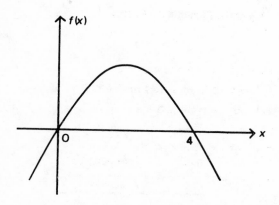

Specimen Questions with Solutions

It might be of interest to pursue the function $f(x)$ from the above for

since $f'(x) = Kx(4-x)$

$$= 4Kx - Kx^2$$

then $f(x) = 2Kx^2 - \dfrac{Kx^3}{3} + c$

We know that $c = 0$ because the graph of $f(x)$ cuts the $f(x)$ axis at the origin

Thus $f(x) = 2Kx^2 - \dfrac{Kx^3}{3}$

We also know that when $x = 4$ $f(x) = \dfrac{32}{3}$

$$\dfrac{32}{3} = 32K - \dfrac{64K}{3}$$

$$\Leftrightarrow \quad \dfrac{1}{3} = K - \dfrac{2K}{3}$$

$$\Leftrightarrow \quad K = 1$$

Thus $f(x) = 2x^2 - \dfrac{x^3}{3}$

$$= \dfrac{x^2}{3}(6-x)$$

15. A sequence $\{u_r; r \in Z\}$ is given by the recurrence relation $u_{r+1} = mu_r + c$, where m and c are constants.

Find $m, c,$ u_3 and u_4 when $u_0 = 0, u_1 = 1, u_2 = 5$.

Solution:

$u_1 = mu_0 + c \quad \Leftrightarrow \quad 1 = 0 + c \Leftrightarrow c = 1$

$u_2 = mu_1 + 1 \quad \Leftrightarrow \quad 5 = m + 1 \Leftrightarrow m = 4$

$u_3 = 4u_2 + 1 \quad \Leftrightarrow \quad u_3 = 4 \times 5 + 1$
$$= 21$$

$u_4 = 4u_3 + 1 \quad \Leftrightarrow \quad u_4 = 4 \times 21 + 1$
$$= 85 \qquad \text{(see page 6)}$$

Printed and bound in Great Britain by Martin's The Printers